HOCKEY HALL OF FAME

HEROES

SCORERS, GOALIES AND DEFENSEMEN

HOCKEY HALL OF FAME

HEROES

SCORERS, GOALIES AND DEFENSEMEN

ERIC ZWEIG

ILLUSTRATIONS BY
GEORGE TODOROVIC

FIREFLY BOOKS

For James. A friend and a mentor. You will be missed.

A FIREFLY BOOK

Published by Firefly Books Ltd. 2016

First printing

Publisher Cataloging-in-Publication Data (U.S.)
A CIP record for this title is available from the Library of Congress

Library and Archives Canada Cataloguing in Publication
A CIP record for this title is available from Library and Archives Canada

Published in the United States by
Firefly Books (U.S.) Inc.
P.O. Box 1338, Ellicott Station
Buffalo, New York 14205

Published in Canada by
Firefly Books Ltd.
50 Staples Avenue, Unit 1
Richmond Hill, Ontario L4B 0A7

Cover and interior design: Kimberley Young
Illustrations: George Todorovic
Creative Direction: Steve Cameron

Printed in Canada

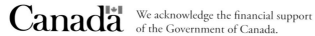

We acknowledge the financial support
of the Government of Canada.

CONTENTS

SUPER SCORERS

DOMINANT DEFENSEMEN

GREAT GOALIES

oday's hockey players are bigger, stronger and faster than players have ever been. But is the game better than it used to be? Maybe. Maybe not. Hockey Hall of Famer Ken Dryden (who's featured in the Great Goalies chapter) once said: "Figure out what year it was when you were 10 years old. That was hockey's best era." I don't think Dryden really means that to be true, but it does explain why older people often say, "the game was better when I was a kid."

Hockey may be its most fun when we're 10 or 12 years old, but that's not the same as saying it's better. I love the history of hockey and one thing that I've discovered is that the game has always been the best it can be. It may look slower in the black-and-white TV footage of Gordie Howe's era, and it may be hard to imagine that even older players like Eddie Shore (whose black-and-white photograph had to be colorized for this book) could possibly have been as exciting to watch as the players in the NHL today. It's true there were no websites back then, or Twitter, or 24-hour sports channels, but if you've read as many old newspaper stories as I have, you come to understand that fans in the old days loved and cared about

the game just as much as the fans do today.

Many of the players who appear in this book — Guy Lafleur, Borje Salming, Bernie Parent — were stars in the NHL around the time that I was 10 years old. I won't lie that the players from that era, and those who began during my teenage years — Wayne Gretzky, Paul Coffey, Grant Fuhr — still hold a special place in my heart. It was a lot of fun for me to pair my heroes with the old-time hockey legends. It's been even more fun to try and match them up with the modern players that boys and girls are watching today; players like Jonathan Toews, Erik Karlsson and Carey Price.

How many of today's NHL stars will ultimately make it to the Hockey Hall of Fame? Only time will tell. Until then, if you're a player yourself, I hope you'll always have fun on the ice no matter where the game takes you. I also hope you're having as much fun watching your own hockey heroes as I did watching mine.

And, of course, I hope you'll enjoy reading this book.

SUPER SCORERS

Wayne Gretzky   CONNOR MCDAVID, JOE MALONE   10

Maurice Richard   PAVEL BURE, NEWSY LALONDE   12

Mike Bossy   BRYAN TROTTIER, CLARK GILLIES, STEVEN STAMKOS   14

Gordie Howe   SID ABEL, TED LINDSAY   16

Bobby Hull   PATRICK KANE, HOWIE MORENZ   18

Brett Hull   ADAM OATES   20

Phil Esposito   ALEX OVECHKIN, FRANK MCGEE   22

Mats Sundin   THE SEDINS, PETER FORSBERG   24

Mario Lemieux   JAROMIR JAGR   26

Guy Lafleur   GILBERT PERREAULT, JEAN BELIVEAU   28

Jari Kurri   PETER STASTNY, TEEMU SELANNE   30

Joe Sakic   JOHN TAVARES, STAN MIKITA   32

Mark Messier   JONATHAN TOEWS   34

Bobby Clarke   BILL BARBER, HARRY BROADBENT   36

Darryl Sittler   FRANK MAHOVLICH, LANNY MCDONALD   38

Steve Yzerman   SIDNEY CROSBY   40

Marcel Dionne   JOHNNY GAUDREAU, CY DENNENY   42

Mike Gartner   YVAN COURNOYER   44

Valeri Kharlamov   SERGEI FEDEROV, EVGENI MALKIN   46

Ron Francis   JOE THORNTON, FRANK BOUCHER   48

Mike Modano   JACK EICHEL, JOE MULLEN   50

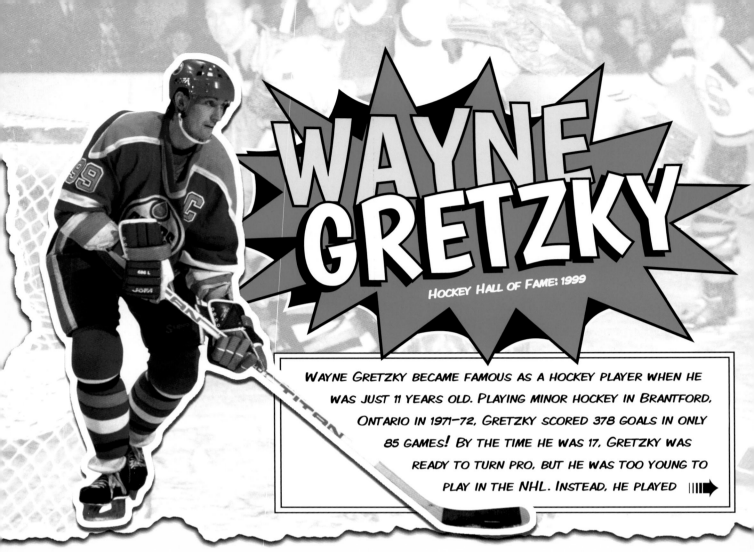

WAYNE GRETZKY

HOCKEY HALL OF FAME: 1999

WAYNE GRETZKY BECAME FAMOUS AS A HOCKEY PLAYER WHEN HE WAS JUST 11 YEARS OLD. PLAYING MINOR HOCKEY IN BRANTFORD, ONTARIO IN 1971–72, GRETZKY SCORED 378 GOALS IN ONLY 85 GAMES! BY THE TIME HE WAS 17, GRETZKY WAS READY TO TURN PRO, BUT HE WAS TOO YOUNG TO PLAY IN THE NHL. INSTEAD, HE PLAYED ⫸

CONNOR McDAVID STARTED skating when he was only three years old. A year later, his parents lied about his age so that he could play hockey with five-year-olds. By the age of 13, it was pretty obvious he was an extra-special player. Like John Tavares and Aaron Ekblad before him, McDavid was allowed to play in the Ontario Hockey League (OHL) when he was 15, a year shy of the minimum age. After three years as a star center with the Erie Otters, the Edmonton Oilers made McDavid the first pick in the 2015 NHL Draft. With blazing speed and Gretzky-like vision, McDavid seems destined for stardom.

MODERN MATCH

CONNOR McDAVID

in a rival league called the World Hockey Association (WHA). Gretzky joined the Edmonton Oilers that year, and even though he was playing against men twice his age, he finished the 1978–79 WHA season third in the league with 110 points.

Before the start of the 1979–80 season, the Oilers joined the NHL and nobody thought Gretzky would succeed. He was a small and skinny kid, and he didn't look like a hockey star. Yet Gretzky made up for his lack of size with his amazing awareness on the ice. Gretzky could spot patterns in the game and find open teammates to create plays that others didn't see. He collected 51 goals and 86 assists for 137 points during his first NHL season. A year later, he broke the NHL record of 152 points when he got 164. And the year after that Gretzky scored 92 goals in one season to smash the old record of 76. In 1985–86, he broke his own records when he set new NHL marks with 163 assists and 215 points!

In just his 11th NHL season, Gretzky scored the 1,851st point of his career. His childhood hero Gordie Howe previously held the record of 1,850 points, and it took him 26 years to set it! Gretzky would later break Howe's record of 801 goals as well, finishing his NHL career with 894 goals and 1,963 assists for 2,857 points — the most in NHL history!

Blast FROM THE Past   JOE MALONE (HHOF: 1950)

Hockey was very different when Joe Malone played over 100 years ago. Forward passing wasn't allowed, so players had to be great puckhandlers. Teams also only carried a few substitutes, meaning the best players often played the whole game and got plenty of chances to score goals. However, very few outscored Joe Malone. During the NHL's first season of 1917–18, Malone netted a league-leading 44 goals for the Montreal Canadiens. He did it in just 20 games! Playing for the Quebec Bulldogs on January 31, 1920, Malone scored seven goals in one game, still an NHL record.

MAURICE RICHARD

HOCKEY HALL OF FAME: 1961

THERE WERE PLAYERS WITH MORE TALENT THAN MAURICE RICHARD. SOME WERE SLICKER SKATERS. OTHERS WERE PRETTIER PLAYMAKERS. BUT VERY FEW HAD THE SAME KNACK FOR THE NET AS THE MAN THEY CALLED THE "ROCKET." IT'S BEEN SAID THAT NO OTHER PLAYER HAS EVER BEEN AS FIERCE OR INTENSE AS MAURICE RICHARD ONCE HE CROSSED THE OPPOSITION'S BLUE LINE. ▐▐▶

He didn't have Maurice Richard's intensity, but Pavel "The Russian Rocket" Bure had speed to burn. He also had incredible balance, which made him hard to knock off the puck. And when he got the puck near the net, he knew what to do with it! Bure began his NHL career with the Vancouver Canucks in 1991–92. No Vancouver player had ever scored 50 goals, but in 1992–93 Bure scored 60! He did it again the following year. Later, with the Florida Panthers, Bure had two more 50-plus-goal seasons. He scored 437 career goals before injuries forced him to retire.

THE RUSSIAN ROCKET

HOCKEY HALL OF FAME: 2012

Pavel BURE

Richard was born and raised in a working-class section of Montreal. When he was starring with the hometown Canadiens in the 1940s and 1950s, many French-Canadian families were struggling to make a living (even in Quebec), and they loved to watch Richard dominate the mostly English-speaking game. Other players often picked on him, breaking the rules to try to slow him down. Many times, Richard fought back, and sometimes his fiery temper got him into trouble. Still, Richard was the heart and soul of the Montreal Canadiens. He played with the team for 18 years from 1942 to 1960 and helped them win the Stanley Cup eight times!

Richard burst out as a star during his second season with the Canadiens in 1943–44. He ranked among the league leaders with 32 goals during the regular season. Then,

in the playoffs, he scored 12 more to lead Montreal to the Stanley Cup. A year later, Richard became the first player in NHL history to score 50 goals in a season, and the season was only 50 games long! It was the first of five times that Richard led the NHL in goals. He went on to become the first NHL player to score 500 career goals. No wonder the NHL awards the Maurice "Rocket" Richard Trophy to the league's top goal scorer.

Blast FROM THE Past   NEWSY LALONDE (HHOF: 1950)

There's a famous saying written on the wall of the Montreal Canadiens dressing room. It's from the World War I poem *In Flanders Field*: "To you from failing hands we throw the torch, be yours to hold it high." It means that as one generation gets old, the traditions are passed on to the next. The tradition of Montreal's great scoring stars begins with Newsy Lalonde, who joined the Canadiens in their first season of 1909–10, seven years before the NHL began. He retired with 440 career goals, and the next closest player was Joe Malone, far behind with 337.

MIKE BOSSY

HOCKEY HALL OF FAME: 1991

ACCORDING TO FAMILY STORIES, MIKE BOSSY'S FATHER GAVE HIM A PLASTIC HOCKEY STICK WHEN BOSSY WAS JUST TWO YEARS OLD. HE WANTED TO SEE WHAT MIGHT HAPPEN. WHAT HAPPENED WAS HIS SON GREW UP TO BE ONE OF THE GREATEST SCORERS IN HOCKEY HISTORY! ▌▌▶

Dynamite Linemates

| BRYAN TROTTIER (HHOF: 1997) | CLARK GILLIES (HHOF: 2002) |

At his first training camp with the New York Islanders, Mike Bossy was placed on a line with Bryan Trottier and Clark Gillies. Trottier had been the rookie of the year in 1974–75. He was a great playmaker who could score goals too. Gillies was a tough customer who could score as well as hit. Together, they were almost unstoppable! The line was known as the "Trio Grande" but was sometimes called the Long Island Electric Company or the Long Island Lighting Company because of the offensive power they supplied.

From the time he started playing hockey, Mike Bossy could always score. In junior hockey, he set a record with 309 goals in just over four seasons. That's an average of nearly 78 goals per year! The Quebec junior league was a rough one, and Bossy hated the violence. He didn't like to fight. Instead, he believed: "If you knock me down, I will get back up and score more goals." Even so, many NHL scouts thought that Bossy wasn't tough enough. It took until the 15th pick in the 1977 NHL Draft before the New York Islanders chose him. Bossy made the team right away, and during the 1977–78 season he became the first rookie in NHL history to score 50 goals! The next year, Bossy led the league with 69 goals. In 1979–80, he helped the Islanders win their first of four straight Stanley Cups!

Heading into the 1980–81 season, Bossy quietly set a challenge for himself. Twenty-three different players had scored 50 goals in a season since Maurice Richard did it first in 1944–45. Still, no one had managed to score 50 goals in just 50 games as Richard had done. That's what Bossy set out to do. Through the first 49 games, he'd scored 48 goals, and with time running out in game number 50, Bossy scored twice in the final five minutes to reach 50 goals! In all, Bossy scored 50 goals a record nine consecutive times in his 10-year NHL career.

Did You Know?

MIKE BOSSY SCORED 573 GOALS IN JUST 752 GAMES. THAT'S AN NHL RECORD SCORING AVERAGE OF .762 GOALS-PER-GAME.

MODERN MATCH
STEVEN STAMKOS

THERE WAS NO waiting around on draft day for Steven Stamkos. Tampa Bay made the slick center the very first choice of the 2008 NHL Draft. He didn't quite have the same fast start as Mike Bossy, but his 23 goals in 2008–09 ranked him third among NHL rookies. In his second season of 2009–10, Stamkos tied Sidney Crosby for the NHL lead with 51 goals.

He alone led the league with 60 goals in 2011–12. Like Bossy, who could fire the puck the moment it reached his stick, Stamkos is known for his lightning-quick "one-timers."

GORDIE HOWE

HOCKEY HALL OF FAME: 1972

GORDIE HOWE, ALSO KNOWN AS "MR. HOCKEY," BEGAN HIS NHL CAREER WITH THE DETROIT RED WINGS IN 1946. HE ENDED IT ALMOST 40 YEARS LATER WITH THE HARTFORD WHALERS IN 1980! IN BETWEEN, HOWE SET RECORDS THAT ONCE SEEMED UNBREAKABLE. HIS NHL TOTALS OF 801 GOALS AND 1,049 ASSISTS FOR 1,850 POINTS ▮▮▮▮➤

FROM THE VAULT

GORDIE'S MITTS

Gordie Howe wore these gloves during the 1952–53 season. That year, he led the NHL with 49 goals. At the time, Maurice Richard was the only player in NHL history who had ever scored 50 goals in one season. Howe also led the NHL with 46 assists in 1952–53, giving him 95 points. That total broke the single-season record of 86 points Howe himself had set two years earlier! Howe also won the Hart Trophy as NHL MVP for the second year in a row in 1952–53.

have now been beaten, but his 1,767 games played remains the most in NHL history.

Standing 6-feet tall (183 cm) and weighing 205 pounds (92 kg), Howe was one of the biggest and strongest players of his era. He wasn't dirty, but he was known for using his elbows to punish opponents that got too rough with him. Howe was also ambidextrous, meaning he could use both hands equally well. He generally shot right handed, but playing at a time when sticks had straight blades, he sometimes switched and shot left-handed to fool the goalie.

Howe started his NHL career slowly, but by his fourth year of 1949–50, he began a streak that saw him finish among the league's top-five scorers for 20 straight seasons! He won the scoring title and was named the league MVP six times each. He also helped Detroit win four Stanley Cups. Still going strong when he was 40 years old, Howe set a career-high with 103 points in 1968–69. He was just the third NHL player ever to reach the 100-point plateau. He still remains the oldest 100-point scorer in NHL history!

Howe retired in 1971 after 25 years with Detroit. Two years later, he made a comeback to play with his sons Mark and Marty in the World Hockey Association (WHA). After six years in the WHA, Howe returned to the NHL for a final season in 1979–80. He was 51 years old!

Did You Know?

GORDIE HOWE LED THE NHL IN SCORING FOUR YEARS IN A ROW FROM 1950–51 TO 1953–54.

Dynamite Linemates

SID ABEL (HHOF: 1969)	TED LINDSAY (HHOF: 1966)

Right winger Gordie Howe first lined up with center Sid Abel and left winger Ted Lindsay during the 1946–47 season. Soon they were the top line in hockey. Writers dubbed the trio "The Production Line" in 1948–49, and they produced plenty of points! Abel led the NHL in goals that year and won the Hart Trophy as league MVP. The next season, Lindsay led the league in scoring. Howe won his first scoring title the following year, making it three straight years the Production Line produced the top scorer in the NHL.

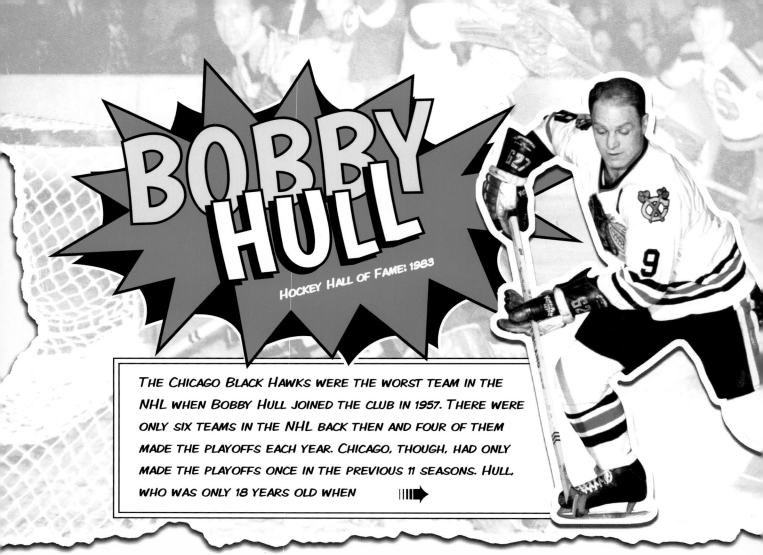

BOBBY HULL

HOCKEY HALL OF FAME: 1983

THE CHICAGO BLACK HAWKS WERE THE WORST TEAM IN THE NHL WHEN BOBBY HULL JOINED THE CLUB IN 1957. THERE WERE ONLY SIX TEAMS IN THE NHL BACK THEN AND FOUR OF THEM MADE THE PLAYOFFS EACH YEAR. CHICAGO, THOUGH, HAD ONLY MADE THE PLAYOFFS ONCE IN THE PREVIOUS 11 SEASONS. HULL, WHO WAS ONLY 18 YEARS OLD WHEN ‖‖▶

THE CHICAGO BLACKHAWKS had missed the playoffs seven times in eight years when they chose Patrick Kane with the very first pick in the 2007 NHL Entry Draft. Kane made the team that year and won the Calder Trophy as the NHL's 2007–08 rookie of the year. Chicago still missed the playoffs, but, just two years later, the Blackhawks were Stanley Cup champions; Kane scored the Cup-winning goal in overtime! Kane has won two more Cups in Chicago, and was named NHL MVP in 2016.

MODERN MATCH
PATRICK KANE

the 1957–58 season started, was the youngest player in the NHL. Chicago missed the playoffs again that year, but Hull and the Hawks were improving. By his third season of 1959–60, Hull was the top scorer in the NHL. One year later, the Black Hawks were Stanley Cup champions.

Hull was the most exciting scorer the NHL had seen in years. He was the fastest skater in the league and his huge, bulging biceps were bigger than the heavyweight boxing champions of the day. Hull used those powerful muscles — and a huge curve in the blade of his stick — to launch unbelievable slap shots. The tools used to measure the speed of shots weren't as good as they are today, but Hull's slapper was said to reach nearly 120 miles per hour (almost 200 kph)!

Maurice Richard became the first player

Did You Know?

WITH HIS BLAZING SPEED, POWERFUL SHOT AND BLONDE GOOD LOOKS, BOBBY HULL WAS KNOWN AS "THE GOLDEN JET."

to score 50 goals in a season when he collected his 50th goal in the 50th and final game of the 1944–45 season. Even after the NHL extended the season to 70 games, only Montreal's Bernie Geoffrion, in 1960–61, was able to score 50 goals. But Bobby Hull became the league's third 50-goal man in 1961–62. In 1965–66, Hull set a new record with 54 goals. He upped that to 58 in 1968–69. That season also marked the seventh time that Hull was the NHL's top goal-scorer. That's a record nobody has beaten.

HOWIE MORENZ (HHOF: 1945)   Blast FROM THE Past

Bobby Hull's blazing speed was often compared to that of the speedy Howie Morenz, the NHL's top offensive star of the 1920s and early 1930s. Morenz joined the Montreal Canadiens for the 1923–24 season and promptly led them to the Stanley Cup. They won it again in 1929–30 and 1930–31. Morenz led the league in points twice and was the first player in history to win the Hart Trophy as MVP three times. Still, it was his speed that really wowed people. It earned him nicknames like the "Canadien Comet," the "Mitchell Meteor" and the "Stratford Streak."

BRETT HULL

HOCKEY HALL OF FAME: 2009

IT TAKES PLENTY OF PRACTICE TO MAKE IT TO THE NHL. IT ALSO HELPS IF HOCKEY TALENT RUNS IN THE FAMILY. THERE HAVE BEEN NEARLY 300 SETS OF BROTHERS WHO'VE MADE IT TO THE NHL, AND MORE THAN 100 FATHERS AND SONS. BOBBY HULL HAD A BROTHER ▐▐▐▶

Dynamite Linemates

ADAM OATES (HHOF: 2012)

Adam Oates began his career in Detroit before joining Brett Hull in St. Louis in 1989–90. Hull needed someone to feed him the puck, and Oates was a brilliant playmaker. The two stars made an instant connection and rocketed up the scoring charts together! Hull and Oates were nearly unstoppable, and in a little less than three seasons in St. Louis the playmaker posted 228 assists! Traded to Boston, Oates led the NHL with 97 assists and posted career-best marks of 45 goals and 142 points in 1992–93.

named Dennis who scored 303 goals in his NHL career, but it was Bobby's son Brett who would join him in the Hockey Hall of Fame.

It was obvious that Brett Hull had heaps of talent. He piled up plenty of goals on his way to the NHL, but he didn't come across as a hard worker. Many hockey experts thought he was slow and lazy. Calgary picked him late in the 1984 NHL Draft, but barely played him before trading him to St. Louis. When Hull joined the Blues, everything suddenly came together. He scored 41 goals during his first full season in St. Louis in 1988–89. The next year, he led the NHL with 72 goals. Hull led the league again in 1990–91. His 86 goals that year marked the third highest single-season total ever scored in the NHL! He won the Hart Trophy as the league's most valuable player, making him and Bobby the only father-and-son MVPs in NHL history. "The Golden Brett" led the league for the third straight year with 70 more goals in 1991–92. After leaving St. Louis in 1998, Hull won the Stanley Cup with Dallas and then Detroit.

Like his father Bobby, Brett Hull had a strong shot, but what made him so dangerous was his quick release. Brett had a knack for finding open spaces on the ice. Once he slipped into a gap, and a teammate passed him the puck, it was on its way to the net in a flash!

Did You Know?

BRETT HULL SCORED 741 GOALS DURING HIS 20 SEASONS IN THE NHL HE WAS THE SIXTH PLAYER IN LEAGUE HISTORY TO TOP 700 GOALS.

BRETT'S BLUE THREADS

Brett Hull wore this jersey with the St. Louis Blues during the 1989–90 season. That year he led the league with 72 goals and became a superstar. It was the first of three straight seasons that Hull led the league in goals, and the first of five years in a row that he scored more than 50! Brett and Bobby Hull are the only father and son to have scored 50 goals in an NHL season. They're also the only ones to score 500 goals in their careers. In fact, they both scored more than 600!

FROM THE VAULT

PHIL ESPOSITO

HOCKEY HALL OF FAME: 1984

PHIL ESPOSITO COULD ALWAYS PUT THE PUCK IN THE NET. HE JUST DIDN'T LOOK GRACEFUL DOING IT. "ESPO" BEGAN HIS NHL CAREER WITH THE CHICAGO BLACK HAWKS DURING THE 1963–64 SEASON. HE HAD THREE SEASONS IN CHICAGO WITH MORE THAN 20 GOALS AND 50 POINTS, BUT THE DECISION MAKERS WHO RAN THE BLACK HAWKS THOUGHT HE WAS SLOW AND LAZY. ▶

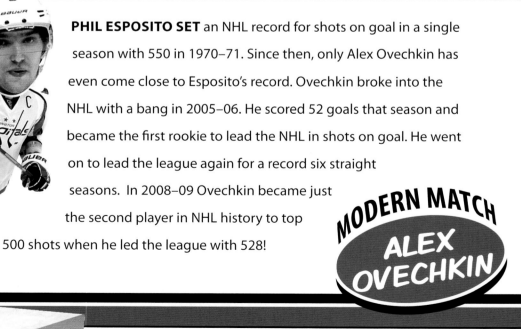

PHIL ESPOSITO SET an NHL record for shots on goal in a single season with 550 in 1970–71. Since then, only Alex Ovechkin has even come close to Esposito's record. Ovechkin broke into the NHL with a bang in 2005–06. He scored 52 goals that season and became the first rookie to lead the NHL in shots on goal. He went on to lead the league again for a record six straight seasons. In 2008–09 Ovechkin became just the second player in NHL history to top 500 shots when he led the league with 528!

MODERN MATCH
ALEX OVECHKIN

Little did they know that he would soon become an NHL superstar! In 1967, Chicago traded Esposito to Boston where he teamed with defenseman Bobby Orr to rewrite the NHL record book.

The Chicago bosses were right about one thing: Espo wasn't a great or fast skater. But he learned to succeed in other ways. Big and strong at 6-foot-1 (185 cm) and 205 pounds (92 kg), he played in front of the other team's net in the area known as "the slot." Standing there, Espo would take passes from his teammates and fire away. During the 1968–69 season, he became the first player in NHL history to top 100 points. He didn't just reach that milestone mark; he shattered it by registering 126 points. Then, in 1969–70, Esposito and Orr helped the Bruins win the Stanley Cup for the first time in 29 years!

Did You Know?

PHIL ESPOSITO WAS THE LEADING SCORER IN THE TOURNAMENT WHEN TEAM CANADA DEFEATED RUSSIA IN THE THRILLING 1972 SUMMIT SERIES.

Esposito had his greatest statistical season in 1970–71. The NHL record for goals in one season was 58, but Espo smashed that when he scored 76! He added 76 assists that year to set another new record with 152 points. He led the league in points again the next three seasons, and had the most goals for four straight years.

Hockey fans were shocked when the Bruins traded Esposito to New York in 1975. He finished out his career with the Rangers, retiring in 1981 with 717 career goals.

Blast FROM THE Past   FRANK McGEE (HHOF: 1945)

Frank McGee was a scoring sensation in the early 1900s. Seasons were short back then, but McGee didn't need a lot of games to pile up a ton of goals. He played only 45 games during four seasons with the Ottawa "Silver Seven" from 1902 to 1906, but scored more than 120 goals! McGee's most amazing feat came on January 16, 1905, when he scored 14 goals in a single Stanley Cup playoff game! Most amazing of all, McGee scored all those goals even though he was blind in one eye because of an injury.

MATS SUNDIN

Hockey Hall of Fame: 2012

MATS SUNDIN WAS THE FIRST EUROPEAN PLAYER TO BE CHOSEN FIRST OVERALL IN THE NHL DRAFT. THE QUEBEC NORDIQUES SELECTED HIM WITH THE TOP PICK IN 1989, AND HE JOINED THE TEAM FOR THE 1990-91 SEASON. SUNDIN SCORED 23 GOALS AS A ROOKIE THAT YEAR. THE NEXT SEASON, ▮▮▮▶

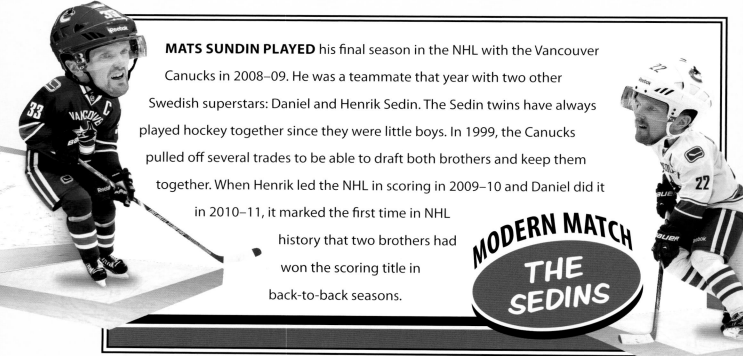

MATS SUNDIN PLAYED his final season in the NHL with the Vancouver Canucks in 2008–09. He was a teammate that year with two other Swedish superstars: Daniel and Henrik Sedin. The Sedin twins have always played hockey together since they were little boys. In 1999, the Canucks pulled off several trades to be able to draft both brothers and keep them together. When Henrik led the NHL in scoring in 2009–10 and Daniel did it in 2010–11, it marked the first time in NHL history that two brothers had won the scoring title in back-to-back seasons.

MODERN MATCH
THE SEDINS

he had 33. In his third season of 1992–93, Sundin established career highs with 47 goals, 67 assists and 114 points.

Sundin was traded to Toronto in 1994. The Maple Leafs gave up fan favorite Wendel Clark to get him, so Sundin knew he was coming into a pressure-packed situation. He responded by leading the Maple Leafs in scoring in 1994–95. Sundin would be the team's top scorer for eight straight seasons. In all, he played 13 seasons in Toronto and led the team in scoring 12 times! He holds the team record for most goals with 420 and most points with 987.

Sundin was named captain of the Maple Leafs in 1997–98. Once again, he was replacing a fan favorite — this time, Doug Gilmour. Gilmour had been a feisty player that the fans loved because he looked like he was giving 110 percent all the time. Sundin, on the other

hand, played a calm, quiet game, and though his teammates always respected him, many fans were never as sure. Still, Sundin continued to play well. In 2001–02, he finished fourth in NHL scoring, which was the highest ranking of his career.

In all, Sundin played 18 seasons in the NHL. He never won the Stanley Cup, but he did have great success in international hockey. Sundin represented Sweden many times. He won World Championships in 1991, 1992 and 1998. In 2002, he was the top scorer at the Olympics. In 2006 he won an Olympic gold medal!

Did You Know?

ON OCTOBER 14, 2006, MATS SUNDIN SCORED THREE GOALS, INCLUDING THE GAME-WINNER IN OVERTIME, TO REACH 500 NHL GOALS.

HOW SWEDE IT IS

Peter Forsberg was only 21 years old when he scored the gold medal-winning goal for Sweden at the 1994 Olympics with an amazing shootout move. He entered the NHL in 1994–95 and won the Calder Trophy as best rookie. A year later, Forsberg collected 116 points and helped the Colorado Avalanche win their first Stanley Cup. He helped them win the Cup again in 2001 and led the NHL in scoring in 2002–03. Swedish players were often accused of lacking toughness, but Forsberg played a very rugged game. Sadly, several serious injuries cut his career short.

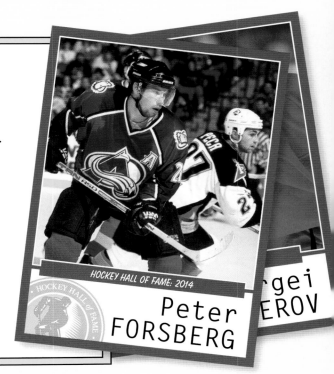

HOCKEY HALL OF FAME: 2014

Peter FORSBERG

gei EROV

MARIO LEMIEUX

HOCKEY HALL OF FAME: 1997

HOCKEY CAME EASILY TO MARIO LEMIEUX. MAYBE TOO EASILY. WHEN HE WAS ONLY FOUR, LEMIEUX COULD DEKE OUT GOALIES THE WAY HIS NHL HEROES DID. BY THE TIME HE WAS SIX, BIG CROWDS GATHERED AT HIS GAMES. AND AT 18, LEMIEUX SET NEW RECORDS IN THE QUEBEC MAJOR JUNIOR HOCKEY LEAGUE. IN 70 GAMES THE GIFTED

FROM THE VAULT

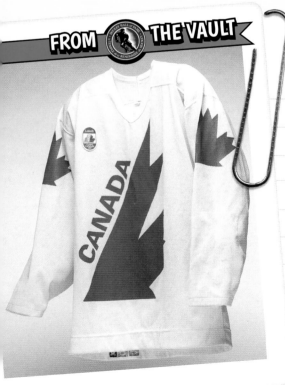

OH CANADA!

Mario Lemieux wore this jersey during the 1987 Canada Cup tournament. At 6-foot-4 (193 cm) and 230 pounds (104 kg), Lemieux was blessed with size and talent. But even with all his skill, he needed to show he had the dedication to work hard and play with the best. Playing alongside Wayne Gretzky and other top talent at the Canada Cup, Lemieux showed he was ready, leading the way with 11 goals in nine games. When Gretzky set him up for the tournament-winning goal with just 1:26 remaining in the final game, it instantly became one of the greatest moments in Canadian hockey history.

goal scorer netted 133 goals and added 149 assists for a whopping 282 points! That's an average of over four points per game!

The Pittsburgh Penguins made Lemieux the first pick in the 1984 NHL Draft. That next season, 1984–85, on his first shift in his first NHL game, Lemieux raced end-to-end to score his first goal on his very first shot! Lemieux had so much talent, he didn't seem to work very hard. He topped 100 points in each of his first four NHL seasons, but people always wondered about his dedication to the game. When Lemieux finally developed the work ethic to go along with his talent, he became one of the greatest players in hockey history.

Lemieux won his first NHL scoring title in 1987–88. The next year, he won it again with a career-high 85 goals, 114 assists, and 199 points. Nobody but Wayne Gretzky has ever had a better season. In all, Lemieux led the NHL in scoring six times. He won the Hart Trophy as MVP three times and led Pittsburgh to the Stanley Cup in 1991 and 1992. Lemieux did it all despite a serious back injury. He even had to overcome cancer during his career. Lemieux retired in 1997 and soon became a part owner of the Penguins. He made a spectacular comeback with Pittsburgh three years later and also helped Team Canada win an Olympic gold medal in 2002.

Did You Know?

IN ENGLISH, MARIO LEMIEUX'S LAST NAME TRANSLATES AS "THE BEST." HE WAS CERTAINLY ONE OF THE BEST PLAYERS EVER.

Dynamite Linemates

JAROMIR JAGR

Playing in his 22nd season in the NHL in 2015–16, Jaromir Jagr continues to climb the NHL scoring charts. He's one of only seven players to top 700 goals and one of only four with more than 1,800 points. He's also the all-time leader in game-winning goals. Jagr's numbers would be even more amazing if he hadn't left the NHL to play in Russia for three seasons. Jagr was a rookie way back in 1990–91 and was a teammate of Mario Lemieux in Pittsburgh for many years. Interestingly, the letters in Jaromir can be re-arranged to spell "Mario Jr."

GUY LAFLEUR

Hockey Hall of Fame: 1988

Plenty of rookies reach the NHL with high expectations. That's especially true for those players who are chosen first in the NHL Draft, like Guy Lafleur was in 1971. Lafleur wasn't just expected to become a superstar with the Montreal Canadiens, he was expected to replace a legend: Jean Beliveau had retired in the spring ▶

HOCKEY HALL OF FAME: 1990

Gilbert
PERREAULT

FRENCH CONNECTION

Gilbert Perreault was a superstar junior player in Montreal. He, along with Guy Lafleur and Marcel Dionne, represented the next wave of French talent to hit the NHL. Perreault made the NHL before the others, as the first overall pick in 1970 for the expansion Buffalo Sabres, making him the first-ever member of the team. He broke rookie-scoring records that year and set every important team-scoring record during his 17 seasons with Buffalo. For years, Perreault played on a line with Quebec-born teammates Richard Martin and Rene Robert. They were known as "The French Connection."

of 1971 after leading the Canadiens to the Stanley Cup for the tenth time in his 20-year career.

Lafleur scored 29 goals as a rookie for Montreal in 1971–72, but he was still considered a disappointment. His offensive totals dropped over the next two seasons and fans began to wonder if the Canadiens had made a mistake. Players didn't have to wear helmets in the NHL during the 1970s, and before the 1974–75 season Lafleur decided to take his helmet off. He thought that if he was forced to play a little bit scared, it might help his game. Maybe it was just a coincidence, but that year, Lafleur (whose name means "the flower") finally blossomed. He was second in the NHL with 53 goals and was fourth in points with 119. For the next few years, Lafleur was the best player in the NHL. He had six straight

50-goal seasons and was named a First Team All-Star at right wing six times. He led the NHL in scoring three years in a row from 1975–76 through 1977–78 and won the Hart Trophy as MVP twice. Lafleur also helped the Canadiens win the Stanley Cup for four straight years from 1976 to 1979.

During his glory days with the Canadiens, just the sight of the speedy Lafleur, flying down the ice at the Montreal Forum with his long, blonde hair blowing in the breeze, was enough to make fans leap to their feet!

Blast FROM THE Past   JEAN BELIVEAU

Jean Beliveau was Guy Lafleur's boyhood hero. At 6-foot-3 (191 cm) and 205 pounds (93 kg), Beliveau was a big man who played hockey with power and grace. He led the NHL in goals twice and assists twice. He also won one scoring title and finished among the top 10 in scoring 11 other times. Beliveau wore No. 4 for the Canadiens. When Guy Lafleur joined the team, he asked Beliveau for permission to wear his number. Knowing the pressure Lafleur would be under, Beliveau told him to pick his own number (No. 10) and make that famous by himself.

HOCKEY HALL OF FAME: 1972

JARI KURRI

HOCKEY HALL OF FAME: 2001

GROWING UP IN FINLAND, JARI KURRI DIDN'T KNOW VERY MUCH ABOUT THE NHL. BACK THEN, NHL GAMES WEREN'T SHOWN ON TV IN FINLAND, AND THERE WASN'T MUCH COVERAGE IN FINNISH NEWSPAPERS. KURRI PLAYED MANY DIFFERENT SPORTS, BUT WHEN HE WAS 15 HE DECIDED TO CONCENTRATE ON HOCKEY BECAUSE HIS FRIENDS ▶

Parallel Playmaker

PETER STASTNY   (HHOF: 1998)

In the 1980s, players from Russia and Czechoslovakia (today, the Czech Republic and Slovakia) were not allowed to leave to join the NHL. In the summer of 1980, Peter Stastny and his brother Anton snuck away from Czechoslovakia to play in the NHL. Another brother named Marian joined them the next year. Peter Stastny had been a top star in Europe, but he was even better in North America. He had 109 points as an NHL rookie in 1980–81 and would top 100 points six more times! During the 1980s, only Wayne Gretzky scored more points than Stastny.

were playing it. Soon, he was one of Finland's top young stars. In 1978, Kurri scored the gold medal–winning goal in overtime at the European Junior Championship. Two years later, in 1980, Kurri helped Finland win a silver medal at the World Junior Championship. His performance there earned him a spot on the 1980 Finnish Olympic team.

The Edmonton Oilers chose Kurri in the fourth round of the 1980 NHL Draft. During the 1980–81 season, he began playing right wing on a line with Wayne Gretzky. Kurri was a good defensive forward, but he also had a very accurate shot. He began piling up points as he cashed in the perfect passes he got from Gretzky. Kurri had his first 50-goal season in 1983–84 and helped Edmonton win the Stanley Cup that year. It was the first of five Stanley Cup victories for the Oilers over a seven-year stretch!

Kurri scored a career-high 71 goals in 1984–85. Gretzky led the NHL with 73 that season, making him and Kurri the only two teammates in league history to top 70 goals! When the Oilers won the Stanley Cup that season, Kurri tied an NHL record with 19 goals in the playoffs. He led the NHL with 68 goals in 1985–86.

Kurri was traded by Edmonton in 1990, and he retired in 1998. At the time, his 601 career goals were the most by a player from Europe.

Did You Know?

JARI KURRI HAD 12 GOALS IN THE 1985 CONFERENCE FINALS TO SET A PLAYOFF RECORD FOR THE MOST GOALS IN A SINGLE SERIES. THE RECORD HAS NEVER BEEN BROKEN.

THE RECORD BREAKER

Hardly anyone had heard of Teemu Selanne when the Winnipeg Jets drafted him 10th overall in 1988. Selanne stayed in Finland to play hockey there for the next four years and didn't join the Jets until the 1992–93 season. He was worth the wait. Selanne shattered the rookie scoring record with 76 goals (which also led the league) and added 56 assists for 132 points! His blazing speed and scoring skill earned him the nickname "The Finnish Flash." Selanne led the NHL in goals two more times and retired with 684 to surpass Jari Kurri as the all-time scoring leader from Finland.

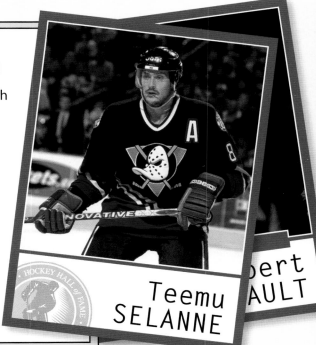

Teemu SELANNE

JOE SAKIC

Hockey Hall of Fame: 2012

Joe Sakic played 20 NHL seasons, all with the same organization but in two different cities. He began his career in 1988-89 with the Quebec Nordiques. After seven seasons, the Nordiques moved to Denver and became the Colorado Avalanche. ▐▐▶

JOHN TAVARES WAS ready to play junior hockey when he was only 14 years old. The rules in the Ontario Hockey League (OHL) said a player had to be 15 to be drafted, but a new rule was passed for Tavares. In his first year in the OHL in 2005–06, Tavares was named rookie of the year. He went on to set a league scoring record with 215 goals in his four-year junior career. In 2009, the New York Islanders chose Tavares first in the NHL Draft. He's gone on to become one of the NHL's top young stars. In 2014 Tavares won an Olympic gold medal with Team Canada!

MODERN MATCH
JOHN TAVARES

He spent 13 more years with the team there. Sakic was a quiet superstar who liked to let his skill speak for itself. It meant he didn't always get the attention he deserved, but when he retired in 2009, he was one of just seven players in NHL history with over 600 goals and more than 1,000 assists.

Sakic was only four years old when he decided he wanted to make hockey his career. Lots of children say they want to be hockey stars, but not very many ever make it. Sakic clearly had the talent and the dedication to keep at it.

Did You Know?

JOE SAKIC HOLDS THE ALL-TIME NHL RECORD FOR THE MOST PLAYOFF OVERTIME GOALS WITH EIGHT IN HIS CAREER.

At 17, he was the rookie of the year in the Western Hockey League. The next season, he was the league's top scorer. A year after that, he was playing in the NHL.

In just his second season of 1989–90, Sakic cracked the top 10 in NHL scoring. It was the first of ten times he would do that. It was also his first of six seasons with 100-or-more points. Still, the Nordiques struggled just to make the playoffs each year. Then, when the team moved to Colorado in 1995–96, success came instantly. Sakic set career highs with 69 assists and 120 points that season and led Colorado to the Stanley Cup. Five years later, Sakic scored a career-high 54 goals and led Colorado to the Stanley Cup again! Sakic was the playoff MVP in 1996. In 2001, he won the Hart Trophy as the most valuable player in the whole league.

Blast FROM THE Past   STAN MIKITA

Stan Mikita spent his entire 22-year career with the Chicago Black Hawks from 1958 to 1980. Early in his career, Mikita got lots of penalties. When he realized he was setting a bad example for his daughter, he decided to clean up his game. Mikita had already led the NHL in scoring twice. Then, in 1966–67, he became the first player to win three major awards in one season. In addition to the Art Ross Trophy for scoring and the Hart Trophy as MVP, he also won the Lady Byng Trophy for sportsmanship. He won all three trophies again in 1967–68.

HOCKEY HALL OF FAME: 1983

MARK MESSIER

HOCKEY HALL OF FAME: 2007

DOUG MESSIER WAS A MINOR-PRO DEFENSEMAN IN THE 1960s. HE WAS GOOD, BUT NEVER MADE THE NHL. HE TAUGHT HIS SON MARK ABOUT THE KIND OF HARD WORK IT TOOK TO MAKE IT AS A PRO HOCKEY PLAYER. MARK NOT ONLY MADE THE NHL, BUT HE HAD ONE OF THE GREATEST CAREERS IN NHL HISTORY! HIS TEAMMATES ALWAYS SAW HOW HARD HE WORKED TO ▐▐▐▶

FROM THE VAULT

THE CAPTAIN'S JERSEY

Mark Messier wore this jersey during Oilers' home games in the 1990 Stanley Cup Final. Most people predicted a tight battle between Edmonton and Boston that year, but the Oilers beat the Bruins in five games. It was their fifth Stanley Cup victory in seven years, but their only one without Wayne Gretzky. Game 1 in the 1990 series went until 15:13 of triple overtime before the Oilers finally won it. It's the longest game in the history of the Stanley Cup Final.

succeed, and it made them work harder too. That's what made Messier such a great leader.

Mark was a late bloomer, but in 1982–83, his fourth professional season, he had a breakout year for the Edmonton Oilers and scored 50 goals. When the Oilers won the Stanley Cup for the first time in 1983–84, Messier was the playoff MVP. Wayne Gretzky was the biggest star on those Edmonton teams, but when he was traded after their fourth Stanley Cup victory in 1987–88, Messier was named captain. The Oilers won the Stanley Cup again (Messier's fifth) in 1989–90. That year Messier notched 84 assists and 129 points and won the Hart Trophy as the NHL's most valuable player.

At the start of the 1991–92 season, Messier was traded to the New York

Did You Know?

MARK MESSIER PLAYED 1,756 GAMES IN HIS CAREER AND HAD 1,887 POINTS. BOTH TOTALS RANK SECOND IN NHL HISTORY.

Rangers. He won the Hart Trophy that season too, but what Ranger fans really wanted was the Stanley Cup. Their team hadn't won it since 1940. In 1993–94, Messier delivered the long-awaited victory. He scored the winning goal in Game 7 of the final and became the only player in NHL history to captain two different teams to the Stanley Cup!

In his career, Messier topped 100 points six times. He played both left wing and center and is the only player in NHL history to be selected a First Team All-Star at both positions.

WHEN JONATHAN TOEWS became captain of the Chicago Blackhawks in 2008–09, he was only 20 years old. It was just his second season, but Toews was already a team leader and intense player, earning him the nickname, "Captain Serious." In 2009–10, Toews led the Blackhawks to their first Stanley Cup in 49 years and was named the MVP of the playoffs! While he isn't the kind of scoring threat that Mark Messier was, he is a talented two-way center who averages nearly 30 goals a season and is great in the faceoff circle. Toews led Chicago to Stanley Cup wins again in 2013 and 2015.

MODERN MATCH
JONATHAN TOEWS

BOBBY CLARKE

Hockey Hall of Fame: 1987

Bobby Clarke won three league scoring titles in a row playing junior hockey in his hometown of Flin Flon, Manitoba. He should have been one of the top choices in the 1969 NHL Draft. Instead, it took until the second round before the Philadelphia Flyers picked him. Clarke had diabetes, and teams were afraid he ▮▮▮▶

Dynamite Linemates

BILL BARBER (HHOF: 1990)

Bill Barber played left wing and center as a junior with the Kitchener Rangers. When Philadelphia selected him with the seventh pick in the 1972 NHL Draft, they decided to play him at left wing on a line with Bobby Clarke. Barber had good hands and an excellent shot. He was a great match for Clarke's passing skills and led all rookies in 1972–73 with 30 goals. Barber scored a career-high 50 goals in 1975–76. His 420 goals during 12 years with the Flyers remain a team record.

wouldn't be strong enough to play in the NHL. But he never let the disease get in his way. Clarke always took proper care of himself, and he had the drive and determination needed to succeed.

The NHL had expanded in size from six to 12 teams in 1967. The Flyers were one of the six new teams, and Bobby Clarke quickly became their leader. He was named team captain in 1972, and the Flyers built a tough team, known as the "Broad Street Bullies," around Clarke and his rough and tumble game. Philadelphia had plenty of fighters and Clarke and the Bullies took lots of penalties, but they had a lot of skill too. During the 1972–73 season, Clarke became the first player from a 1967 expansion team to score 100 points. He finished with 104, good for second in scoring behind Phil Esposito. More importantly, Clarke won his first Hart Trophy as NHL MVP that year. The Flyers became the first expansion team to win the Stanley Cup when they won back-to-back championships in 1973–74 and 1974–75. Clarke won his second Hart Trophy in 1974–75, and the next year set a career high with 119 points, winning his third MVP award!

Clarke spent his entire playing career with Philadelphia, and he still holds Flyers team records for the most seasons (15), the most games (1,144), the most assists (852) and the most points (1,210).

Did You Know?

BOBBY CLARKE WAS A STRONG TWO-WAY PLAYER. HE WON THE SELKE TROPHY AS THE NHL'S BEST DEFENSIVE FORWARD IN 1982-83.

Blast FROM THE Past HARRY BROADBENT (HHOF: 1962)

Harry "Punch" Broadbent was a high-scoring star who was as tough as he was talented. Broadbent could deke around his opponents, but sometimes he would just skate right over them! Broadbent's pro career, which included time in Montreal and New York, began with the Ottawa Senators in 1912. His best season came in 1921–22. That year, he led the NHL with 32 goals and 46 points in just 24 games played. Broadbent set a record that season that still stands by scoring at least one goal in 16 consecutive games!

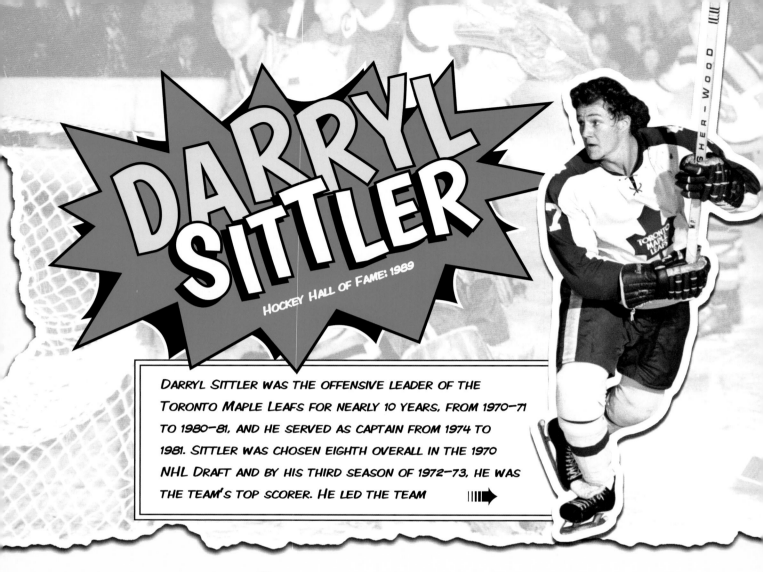

DARRYL SITTLER

HOCKEY HALL OF FAME: 1989

Darryl Sittler was the offensive leader of the Toronto Maple Leafs for nearly 10 years, from 1970–71 to 1980–81, and he served as captain from 1974 to 1981. Sittler was chosen eighth overall in the 1970 NHL Draft and by his third season of 1972–73, he was the team's top scorer. He led the team ▐▐▐▶

FRANK MAHOVLICH **Blast** FROM THE **Past**

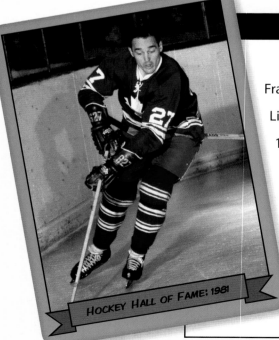

HOCKEY HALL OF FAME: 1981

Frank Mahovlich was Toronto's top scorer for most of the 1960s. Like Darryl Sittler in the 1970s, Mahovlich wore No. 27. During the 1960–61 season, Mahovlich was in a scoring race with Montreal's Bernie Geoffrion to try and become the NHL's second 50-goal scorer. Mahovlich fell just short, but his 48 goals that year remained a Maple Leafs record for 21 years until Rick Vaive scored 54 goals in 1981–82. Mahovlich helped Toronto win the Stanley Cup in 1962, 1963, 1964 and 1967. He later won the Cup again with Montreal in 1971 and 1973.

in scoring six more times and became the first player in Maple Leafs history to hit the 100-point mark. But it is what he did on February 7, 1976, that still has hockey fans talking today.

Toronto was facing Boston that night. The Bruins had won seven in a row, but the Maple Leafs beat them badly and Sittler set a record that has never been broken. He had 10 points in a single game! Midway through the first period, Sittler set up a pair of goals to put Toronto ahead 2–0. He had two more assists and scored three goals of his own in the second period for seven points. The NHL record was eight, and Sittler tied it with his fourth goal of the night 44 seconds into the third period. He broke the record with his fifth goal midway through the third period, then added one more a little bit later. Sittler finished the night with six goals and four assists and Toronto won the game 11–4!

Sittler had another big night two months later. On April 22, 1976, he tied an NHL playoff record with five goals in one game. His best season, however, came in 1977–78 when Sittler set career highs with 45 goals, 72 assists and 117 points. His third-place finish in the scoring race that year marked the first time since the 1945–46 season that a Toronto player had finished as a top-three scorer!

Did You Know?

DARRYL SITTLER SCORED THE WINNING GOAL IN OVERTIME WHEN TEAM CANADA WON THE FIRST CANADA CUP TOURNAMENT IN 1976.

Dynamite Linemates

LANNY MCDONALD (HHOF: 1992)

Lanny McDonald was a junior scoring star in Medicine Hat, Alberta, when Toronto chose him fourth overall in 1973. In his third season with Toronto in 1975–76, the right winger was placed on a line with center Darryl Sittler, and he took off! McDonald jumped from 44 points to 93 that season, and topped 40 goals in each of the next three years. Toronto traded McDonald midway through the 1979–80 season. Two years later, he wound up in Calgary. During the 1982–83 season, McDonald set a Flames record that still stands, by scoring 66 goals!

STEVE YZERMAN

Hockey Hall of Fame: 2009

STEVE YZERMAN LOVED HOCKEY AS A BOY. THE WALLS IN HIS ROOM WERE COVERED WITH POSTERS OF PLAYERS FROM ALL GENERATIONS. YZERMAN LEARNED TO SKATE ON A LAKE NEAR HIS HOMETOWN OF CRANBROOK, BRITISH COLUMBIA. HE BEGAN PLAYING HOCKEY AFTER THE FAMILY MOVED TO THE OTTAWA SUBURB OF NEPEAN, ONTARIO. WHEN HE WAS 18, THE DETROIT RED WINGS CHOSE YZERMAN FOURTH ▸

SIDNEY CROSBY'S NHL debut was even more spectacular than Steve Yzerman's. Chosen first overall by the Pittsburgh Penguins in 2005, he became the youngest player in NHL history (18 years, eight months) to collect 100 points. He was just 19 years old when he won his first NHL scoring title in 2006–07. Crosby was named captain of the Penguins in 2007–08 and helped Pittsburgh win the Stanley Cup in 2009. Crosby has excelled internationally as well, scoring the gold medal-winning goal at the 2010 Olympics. He won a second Olympic gold in 2014 and another Stanley Cup in 2016!

MODERN MATCH
SIDNEY CROSBY

overall in the 1983 NHL Draft. He made the team that year and went on to play 22 seasons for Detroit — that's a long time!

In 1983–84, the 18-year-old Yzerman set Red Wings rookie records with 39 goals and 87 points. He also became the youngest player to play in the NHL All-Star Game. By the time he was 21 he was Detroit's captain, and when he was 22, in 1987–88, Yzerman scored 50 goals and had 102 points. What's more impressive is that he scored all those points in only 64 games! It was the first of six straight seasons that Yzerman registered 100 points or more. Still, when Scotty Bowman became the Red Wings coach in 1993–94, he demanded that the slick scorer improve his defensive skills. Yzerman eventually became one of the league's best defensive forwards, and his two-way play helped Detroit win the

Stanley Cup in 1997. It was the first time the Red Wings had won it in 42 years! Yzerman captained Detroit to Cup wins again in 1998 and 2002.

Injuries slowed him down in his later years, but when Yzerman retired in 2006, he had scored 692 goals. His 1,063 assists broke the team record of 1,023 previously held by Gordie Howe. By then, Yzerman had been captain of the Red Wings for 20 years. That's by far the longest time that any player has worn the "C" in NHL history!

MVP JERSEY

Steve Yzerman wore this jersey for Detroit during the 1988–89 season. That year, Yzerman set Red Wings records with 65 goals, 90 assists and 155 points. Not only was it the greatest offensive season in team history, it was one of the greatest in NHL history too. Only Wayne Gretzky and Mario Lemieux have ever scored more points in a single season than Yzerman did that year. Sportswriters voted for Wayne Gretzky as the winner of the Hart Trophy as NHL MVP that season, but when the players cast their own votes for MVP, they chose Yzerman.

FROM THE VAULT

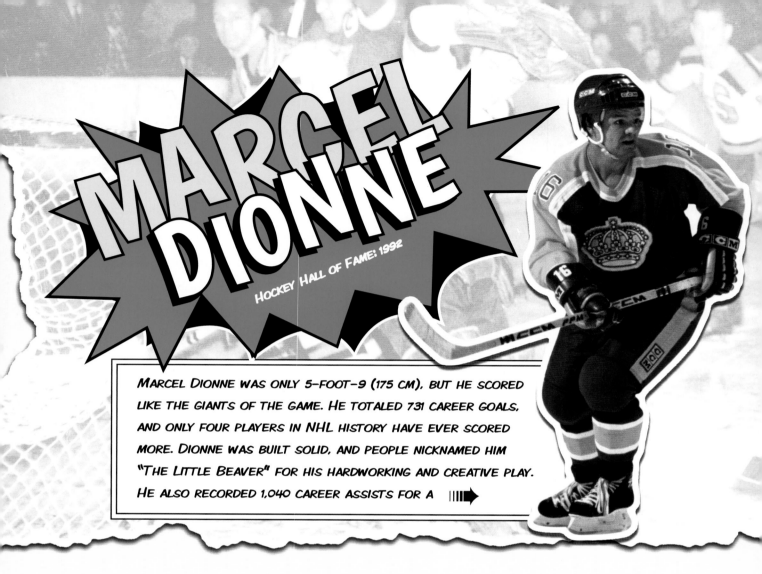

MARCEL DIONNE

Hockey Hall of Fame: 1992

MARCEL DIONNE WAS ONLY 5-FOOT-9 (175 CM), BUT HE SCORED LIKE THE GIANTS OF THE GAME. HE TOTALED 731 CAREER GOALS, AND ONLY FOUR PLAYERS IN NHL HISTORY HAVE EVER SCORED MORE. DIONNE WAS BUILT SOLID, AND PEOPLE NICKNAMED HIM "THE LITTLE BEAVER" FOR HIS HARDWORKING AND CREATIVE PLAY. HE ALSO RECORDED 1,040 CAREER ASSISTS FOR A ▮▮▮▶

SOMETIMES, GOOD THINGS really do come in small packages. The NHL lists Johnny Gaudreau as standing 5-foot-9 (175 cm), but he weighs only 157 pounds (71 kg). Because of his small size, the Calgary Flames waited until the 104th pick in the 2011 NHL Draft before selecting Gaudreau. He spent the next three seasons with Boston College, and in 2013–14 he was the top scorer in all of U.S. college hockey with 80 points in just 40 games. Entering the NHL with the Flames in 2014–15, "Johnny Hockey" was among the top-scoring rookies in the league. Calgary hopes for big things from the small forward.

MODERN MATCH

JOHNNY GAUDREAU

combined total of 1,771 points, which is sixth best in NHL history. Yet, unlike a giant, Marcel Dionne always seemed to be playing in someone else's shadow.

As a junior player before he reached the NHL, Dionne and Guy Lafleur were big rivals. In fact, there were some people with the Montreal Canadiens who wanted Dionne instead of Lafleur. Ultimately, the Canadiens chose Lafleur with the top pick in 1971, and Dionne went to Detroit with the second choice. He set a new rookie record with 77 points that season, but when the time came to hand out the Calder Trophy, Canadiens goalie Ken Dryden was named rookie of the year.

Dionne finished third in NHL scoring with 121 points in 1974–75, but after that season he left Detroit for Los Angeles. The Kings weren't very popular then, so even though Dionne topped 50 goals six times and 100 points on seven more occasions, someone else usually won the NHL's top awards. Even when Dionne did win the NHL scoring title in 1979–80, his victory was unusual. He and Wayne Gretzky both finished the season with 139 points, but Dionne was given the Art Ross Trophy because he'd scored 53 goals to Gretzky's 51. Even so, it was Gretzky who was named league MVP. Dionne's teams never won a championship either, making him probably the best player in NHL history to never get his name on the Stanley Cup.

Did You Know?

IN 1980–81, EACH PLAYER ON THE KINGS' TRIPLE CROWN LINE OF MARCEL DIONNE, CHARLIE SIMMER AND DAVE TAYLOR TOPPED 100 POINTS.

Blast FROM THE Past   CY DENNENY (HHOF: 1959)

Cy Denneny didn't look like an athlete. He was kind of pudgy. He wasn't a great skater either, but Denneny had a hard, accurate shot. Some people even said he could make the puck curve when he shot it. Like Dionne, Denneny was a star player, but it often seemed that someone else was a little bit better. During the NHL's first season of 1917–18, Denneny had a career-high 36 goals in just 20 games but Joe Malone led the league with 44. Denneny won the scoring title in 1923–24, but he finished second five times.

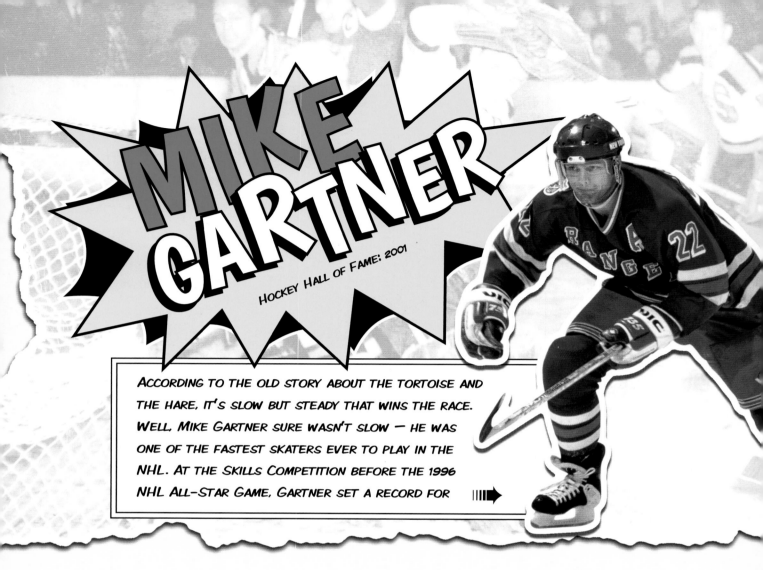

MIKE GARTNER

Hockey Hall of Fame: 2001

According to the old story about the tortoise and the hare, it's slow but steady that wins the race. Well, Mike Gartner sure wasn't slow — he was one of the fastest skaters ever to play in the NHL. At the Skills Competition before the 1996 NHL All-Star Game, Gartner set a record for

Hockey Hall of Fame: 1982

YVAN COURNOYER — Blast from the Past

Yvan Cournoyer played in the NHL from 1963 to 1979. He spent his whole career with the Montreal Canadiens. In those 16 years, he got his name on the Stanley Cup 10 times! Cournoyer was only 5-foot-7 (170 cm), but he was fast. He was nicknamed "The Roadrunner" after the speedy cartoon bird. Cournoyer's speed allowed him to swoop in on loose pucks, and his skill on his skates made it hard for the bigger players to hit him. Cournoyer had 40 goals or more four times in his career. He ranked among the NHL's top goal scorers six times.

the fastest lap around the rink. He made it all the way around the ice in just 13.386 seconds. His record wasn't broken for 20 years! So, Gartner wasn't slow, but he sure was steady. In fact, he may have been the most consistent scorer in hockey history.

Mike Gartner began his career in the World Hockey Association (WHA) in 1978–79. That year, he was the runner-up to Wayne Gretzky for the WHA rookie of the year. The next season, Gartner entered the NHL with the Washington Capitals. He scored 36 goals to set a Washington rookie record that was finally broken by Alex Ovechkin in 2005–06. For Gartner, it was the first of 15 straight seasons in which he scored at least 30 goals. That's a record that's only been matched once, by Jaromir Jagr. Gartner's streak was finally snapped by a strike-shortened season in 1994–95. He only

Did You Know?

DURING THE NINE-AND-A-HALF SEASONS HE PLAYED FOR WASHINGTON, MIKE GARTNER SET OR TIED 12 DIFFERENT TEAM SCORING RECORDS.

got to play in 38 games that year. The next season, he bounced back with 35 goals for the Toronto Maple Leafs. In all, Gartner scored 30 goals or more 17 times in his 19-year career. That's a record that no one has beaten!

Gartner only scored 50 goals once, but he was his team's top goal-scorer nine times. He never led the league, but with his steady performance year after year, Gartner was just the fifth player in NHL history to score more than 700 goals. He had 708 when he retired in 1998.

MIKE'S LID

Mike Gartner wore this helmet during his days with the Washington Capitals. Back then, it was rare for players to wear a visor. Gartner was one of the first big stars to do so. He put it on after he was hit in the eye with a puck during the 1982–83 season. "The doctors have told me I have to wear it," Gartner later explained. "So I do. I wouldn't think of going out there without my pants or my shoulder pads...I have to look at the shield the same way. It's part of my equipment."

FROM THE VAULT

VALERI KHARLAMOV

HOCKEY HALL OF FAME: 2005

VALERI KHARLAMOV NEVER GOT A CHANCE TO PLAY IN THE NHL. STILL, HE BECAME A VERY FAMILIAR NAME TO HOCKEY FANS IN NORTH AMERICA WHEN TEAM CANADA FACED THE RUSSIANS IN THE 1972 SUMMIT SERIES. KHARLAMOV WAS A BRILLIANT PUCKHANDLER AND A FAST SKATER. AT JUST ▐▶

HOCKEY HALL OF FAME: 2015

Sergei FEDEROV

NEXT GENERATION

As part of a new wave of young Russian stars in the late 1980s, Sergei Fedorov's decision to illegally leave the Soviet national team and join the Detroit Red Wings in 1990 pushed Russia to allow players to go to the NHL. Fedorov was an immediate success in Detroit as a great two-way player. He reached a career high with 56 goals and 120 points in 1993–94. He not only won the Hart Trophy as NHL MVP that year, but also the Selke Trophy as the league's best defensive forward — a rare combination!

5-foot-8 (172 cm) and 165 pounds (73 kg), he wasn't very big, but he was strong. He was never afraid to go one-on-one against the world's toughest defensemen.

Kharlamov's hockey talent was obvious when he was just a boy. At 14, he became part of the top club in Russia — Moscow's Central Red Army. By the time he was 20 in 1968, he was playing with the Red Army's best team in the top Russian league.

In 1972, Russia won gold at the Winter Olympics. A few months later, the Russian team played the top Canadian stars from the NHL in a special series of eight exhibition games. Russia had dominated the Olympics and the World Championships for years, but many said it was because NHL players weren't allowed to participate. So, most people in Canada expected the NHL stars to win the Summit Series. They were certainly shocked when Kharlamov scored two goals to lead Russia to a 7–3 win in game one. The series went right down to the wire before Team Canada won it in the final seconds of the final game.

Kharlamov played in 11 World Championships during his career, winning a medal every time, including eight golds, two silvers and one bronze. He also won two golds and one silver in three tries at the Olympics. In regular-season play, Kharlamov and the Red Army won 11 league championships. He had 293 goals and 509 points in 436 games. Sadly, Kharlamov was killed in a car accident in 1981.

Did You Know?

VALERI KHARLAMOV WAS NAMED AN ALL-STAR AT THE WORLD CHAMPIONSHIP TOURNAMENT IN 1972, 1973, 1975 AND 1976.

EVGENI MALKIN WAS the second pick in the 2004 NHL Draft, right behind fellow Russian Alex Ovechkin. When Malkin began his career with Pittsburgh in 2006–07, he set a modern NHL record by scoring goals in his first six games. He went on to win the Calder Trophy as rookie of the year. In 2008–09, Malkin won the NHL scoring title. When Pittsburgh won the Stanley Cup, Malkin also earned the Conn Smythe Trophy as playoff MVP. He won another scoring title in 2011–12. Malkin wears No. 71 for Pittsburgh in tribute to Valeri Kharlamov, whose number was 17.

MODERN MATCH
EVGENI MALKIN

RON FRANCIS

HOCKEY HALL OF FAME: 2007

RON FRANCIS PLAYED 23 SEASONS IN THE NHL FROM 1981 TO 2004. HE WAS A CONSISTENT SCORER WHO HAD 549 CAREER GOALS. AND WHILE HE NEVER HAD MORE THAN 32 GOALS IN HIS BEST YEAR, HE SCORED 20-PLUS GOALS 20 TIMES! ONLY GORDIE HOWE HAS MORE 20-GOAL SEASONS THAN THAT. STILL, SCORING GOALS WASN'T ▮▮▮➡

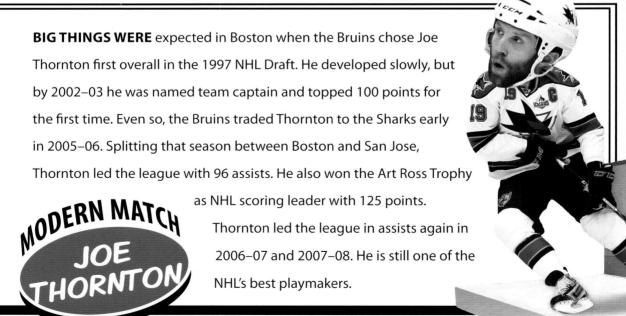

BIG THINGS WERE expected in Boston when the Bruins chose Joe Thornton first overall in the 1997 NHL Draft. He developed slowly, but by 2002–03 he was named team captain and topped 100 points for the first time. Even so, the Bruins traded Thornton to the Sharks early in 2005–06. Splitting that season between Boston and San Jose, Thornton led the league with 96 assists. He also won the Art Ross Trophy as NHL scoring leader with 125 points.

Thornton led the league in assists again in 2006–07 and 2007–08. He is still one of the NHL's best playmakers.

MODERN MATCH
JOE THORNTON

what Francis was known for. He was a playmaker and a defensive forward. Francis ranked among the NHL's top 10 in assists 12 times and led the league twice. By the end of his career, Francis had accumulated 1,249 assists. That ranks him second all-time behind only Wayne Gretzky. He ranks third all-time in games played with 1,731 and fifth in points with 1,798.

Francis began his career with the Hartford Whalers. He was their first choice, fourth overall, in the 1981 NHL Draft and joined the team partway through the 1981–82 season. Francis quickly became one of Hartford's top players, and in his fourth season he was named captain. Soon, the Whalers were a consistent playoff team, though they rarely managed to win even a single round. Late in the 1990–91 season, Francis was traded to Pittsburgh. He took his game to a whole new level

with the Penguins. Centering the team's second line, behind Mario Lemieux and Jaromir Jagr, Francis helped Pittsburgh win the Stanley Cup that year. They won it again in 1991–92. He remained in Pittsburgh until 1998. During the 1997–98 season, Francis' old team from Hartford moved to Carolina and became the Hurricanes. Francis rejoined the team in 1998–99. In all, he spent 16 seasons with the Whalers/Hurricanes. He holds the franchise records for most games (1,186), most goals (382), most assists (793) and most points (1,175).

Did You Know?

IN 2013, RON FRANCIS BECAME THE FIRST HOCKEY PLAYER INDUCTED INTO THE NORTH CAROLINA SPORTS HALL OF FAME.

Blast FROM THE Past   FRANK BOUCHER (HHOF: 1958)

In hockey's early days, passing the puck forward was against the rules. For the 1929–30 season, the NHL finally allowed forward passing in every zone. Before then, no one had ever had more than 18 assists in a season. But that year, Frank Boucher doubled the NHL record to 36 assists. Boucher centered high-scoring brothers Bill and Bun Cook on the New York Rangers' top line. Between 1926–27 and 1934–35, Boucher led the NHL in assists three times and finished second four times. He also won the Lady Byng Trophy for sportsmanship a record seven times!

MIKE MODANO

Hockey Hall of Fame: 2014

DETROIT IS KNOWN AS HOCKEYTOWN, USA, AND IT'S NOT JUST BECAUSE THE RED WINGS ARE ONE OF THE NHL'S OLDEST AND BEST FRANCHISES. IT'S ALSO BECAUSE THE SMALL CITIES AND SUBURBS AROUND DETROIT BOAST SOME OF THE BEST YOUTH HOCKEY PROGRAMS IN THE UNITED STATES. ‖►

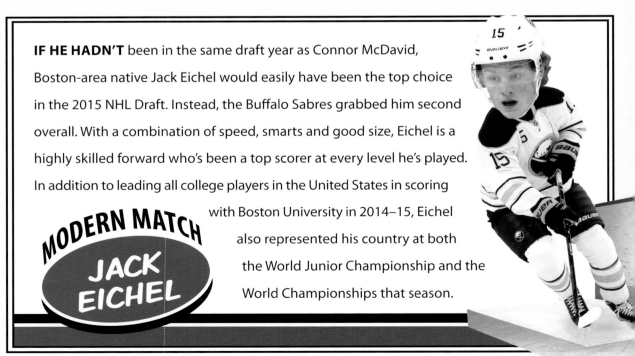

IF HE HADN'T been in the same draft year as Connor McDavid, Boston-area native Jack Eichel would easily have been the top choice in the 2015 NHL Draft. Instead, the Buffalo Sabres grabbed him second overall. With a combination of speed, smarts and good size, Eichel is a highly skilled forward who's been a top scorer at every level he's played. In addition to leading all college players in the United States in scoring with Boston University in 2014–15, Eichel also represented his country at both the World Junior Championship and the World Championships that season.

MODERN MATCH
JACK EICHEL

Mike Modano was a high-scoring midget hockey player in the Detroit area before leaving home in 1986 to play junior hockey in Prince Albert, Saskatchewan. In 1988, Modano became just the second American to be chosen first overall in the NHL Draft. His selection that year by the Minnesota North Stars meant that he'd be moving to the Midwest to play in another U.S. hockey hotbed. Eventually Modano would become the top-scoring American player in NHL history with 561 goals and 1,374 points.

Modano helped the North Stars reach the Stanley Cup Final for the first time in team history in 1990–91 and led the team in scoring over the next two seasons. In 1993–94, the North Stars left Minnesota and became the Dallas Stars. Modano helped win over fans in the new city by scoring a career-high 50 goals

that year. By 1996–97, Dallas was becoming an NHL powerhouse, eventually winning the Stanley Cup in 1999. Modano was captain of the team from 2003 to 2006 and remained in Dallas through the 2009–10 season. Modano then returned to his hometown of Detroit when he joined the Red Wings in 2010–11, but after just one season he signed a one-day contract with Dallas so that he could retire as a Star. During his career, Modano led the Stars in goals scored six times and in points 11 times. He is the all-time franchise leader in nearly every offensive category, including games played (1,459), goals (557), assists (802) and points (1,359).

BORN IN THE USA

Joe Mullen grew up in a rough New York City neighborhood known as Hell's Kitchen. Drugs and crime were a constant problem, but Mullen's family lived close to Madison Square Garden. His love of hockey helped him stay away from the dangers of his neighborhood. Mullen didn't learn to skate until he was 10, but soon he was a high-scoring star in the New York Junior Hockey League. He went on to play 16 seasons in the NHL with St. Louis, Calgary, Pittsburgh and Boston between 1981 and 1997. On March 14, 1997, Mullen became the first American-born player to score 500 goals in the NHL.

HOCKEY HALL OF FAME: 2000

Joe MULLEN

eter BERG

DOMINANT DEFENSEMEN

57

60

75

85

88

BOBBY ORR

HOCKEY HALL OF FAME: 1979

MOST EXPERTS CONSIDER BOBBY ORR TO BE THE GREATEST DEFENSEMAN TO EVER PLAY. MANY EVEN THINK HE WAS THE GREATEST PLAYER OF ALL-TIME! BEFORE BOBBY ORR, THERE HAD BEEN OFFENSIVE-MINDED DEFENSEMEN, BUT NO ONE HAD PLAYED THE WAY ORR DID. HIS SPEEDY SKATING, CREATIVE PASSING AND

MIKE GRANT (HHOF: 1950)  Blast FROM THE Past

Mike Grant may have been hockey's first offensive defenseman. Grant played with the Montreal Victorias in the 1890s! He'd been a champion speed skater as a boy and brought that skill to hockey. After joining the Victorias for the 1893–94 season, Grant's speed on the ice helped turn his team into champions. The Vics won the Stanley Cup from 1895 to 1899, and his rushing style influenced his teammates. In a Stanley Cup game in 1899, Grant's defense partner Graham Drinkwater rushed the puck from end to end in the final seconds to score the winning goal.

his awesome offensive skills changed the way hockey was played forever. Very soon, every team was looking to add their own Bobby Orr.

NHL scouts first noticed Orr when he was only 12 years old. By the time he was 18, he had joined the Boston Bruins in the NHL. Orr was easily the most exciting new player of 1966–67, and his unique style won him the Calder Trophy as the NHL rookie of the year. The next year, he won the Norris Trophy as the NHL's best defenseman. He won that award eight years in a row!

Orr set a record for defensemen when he scored 21 goals in 1968–69, then he smashed it with 33 goals in 1969–70. That year, he recorded 120 points, which made Orr the first defenseman ever to top 100 points and the first defenseman to lead the entire league in scoring. He is still the only defenseman in NHL history to win the scoring title, and he did it twice! Orr

was no slouch on defense either. He wasn't a big hitter, but his skating and positioning was so strong that offensive players rarely got around him.

Orr scored the winning goal in overtime to give Boston the Stanley Cup in 1970 and he helped them win it again in 1972. Sadly, Orr suffered a series of serious knee injuries that forced him to retire when he was only 30 years old. He barely played nine full seasons in the NHL.

Did You Know?

BOBBY ORR WAS THE FIRST PLAYER TO WIN THE HART TROPHY AS NHL MVP THREE YEARS IN A ROW, FROM 1969–70 TO 1971–72.

THE NORRIS TROPHY

The NHL's annual award for best defenseman is officially known as the James Norris Memorial Trophy. Most people call it the Norris Trophy. But who was James Norris? Norris grew up in Montreal and later became a wealthy businessman in Chicago. In 1932, he bought the NHL team in Detroit and changed its name from Falcons to Red Wings. When James Norris died in 1952, his children wanted to do something special to honor him. Before the start of the 1953–54 season, they donated a trophy in his name. Five-time winner Raymond Bourque can be seen holding the trophy at right.

NORRIS TROPHY: 1987, 1988, 1990, 1991, 1994

Raymond BOURQUE

klas TROM

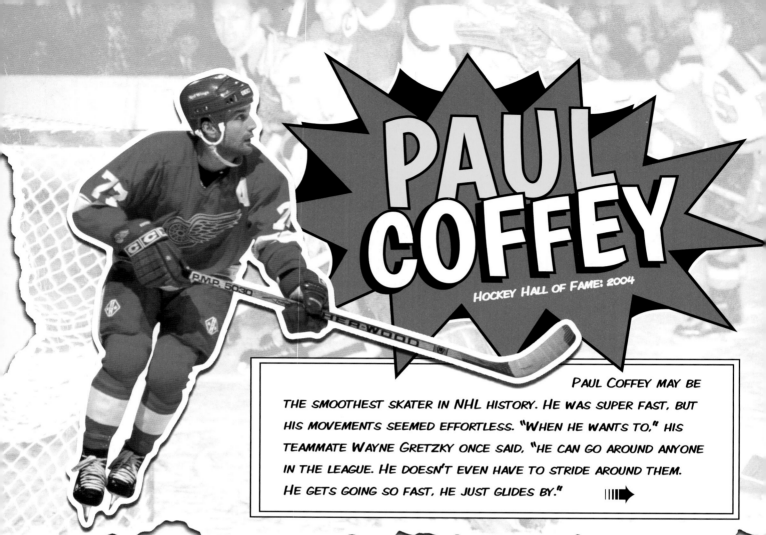

PAUL COFFEY

HOCKEY HALL OF FAME: 2004

PAUL COFFEY MAY BE THE SMOOTHEST SKATER IN NHL HISTORY. HE WAS SUPER FAST, BUT HIS MOVEMENTS SEEMED EFFORTLESS. "WHEN HE WANTS TO," HIS TEAMMATE WAYNE GRETZKY ONCE SAID, "HE CAN GO AROUND ANYONE IN THE LEAGUE. HE DOESN'T EVEN HAVE TO STRIDE AROUND THEM. HE GETS GOING SO FAST, HE JUST GLIDES BY."

KING CLANCY (HHOF: 1958)

Blast FROM THE Past

King Clancy began his NHL career with the Ottawa Senators in 1921–22. Ottawa was one of the best teams in hockey at the time and Clancy helped them win the Stanley Cup in 1923 and 1927. At 5-foot-7 (170 cm) and only 155 pounds (70 kg) Clancy was small for an NHL defenseman, but he never backed down from bigger opponents. Like Coffey, he was one of the top-scoring defensemen of his day. Before the 1930–31 season, Clancy was traded to Toronto for $35,000 and two players. At the time, it was the most expensive trade in hockey history!

The Edmonton Oilers chose Coffey sixth overall in the 1980 NHL Draft. Many teams like to leave their young defensemen in junior hockey or the minors to gain experience. Not the Oilers! They were a young team on the rise and they wanted all their top stars working together right away in the NHL. Coffey's numbers were nothing special as a rookie in 1980–81, but by the 1981–82 season, he and the Oilers were ready to take off. Coffey's quick skating made him a perfect fit with Gretzky and the high-flying offense in Edmonton. By the 1983–84 season, the Oilers were Stanley Cup champions and Coffey had joined Bobby Orr as the only defensemen in NHL history to score 40 goals in a single season. In 1985–86, Coffey almost became the first defenseman to score 50! He fell just short with 48, though he did break Orr's record of 46. Coffey's career-high 138 points that season were just one behind Orr's record total of

139. Before the 1987–88 season, Edmonton traded Coffey to Pittsburgh where he got to team up with another superstar, Mario Lemieux.

Great as he was as a goal scorer, Coffey was even more dangerous setting up his teammates. He was often among the league's leaders in assists and was the first defenseman in NHL history to top 1,000 in his career. Coffey's lifetime total of 1,135 assists ranks him fifth among all players in NHL history.

Did You Know?

PAUL COFFEY WON THREE STANLEY CUPS WITH EDMONTON AND ONE WITH PITTSBURGH. HE ALSO WON THE NORRIS TROPHY TWICE WITH EDMONTON AND ONCE WITH DETROIT.

WHEN MORGAN RIELLY was in junior hockey, he said that if he could have supper with anyone, he'd pick Paul Coffey. "I've always liked him and looked up to him," Rielly said. When the smooth-skating Coffey was inducted into Canada's Sports Hall of Fame in 2015, he was asked about the skaters in the NHL that impress him. "I like the kid in Toronto, Rielly … He can go." Like Coffey, Rielly was an early pick in the first round of the NHL Draft, selected fifth overall by the Maple Leafs in 2012. Toronto fans hope Rielly will become a big star, just like Coffey.

MODERN MATCH
MORGAN RIELLY

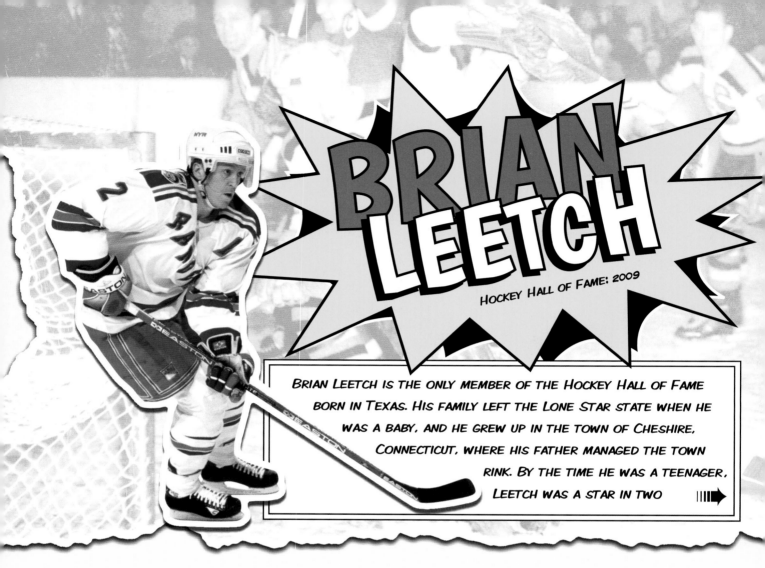

BRIAN LEETCH

HOCKEY HALL OF FAME: 2009

BRIAN LEETCH IS THE ONLY MEMBER OF THE HOCKEY HALL OF FAME BORN IN TEXAS. HIS FAMILY LEFT THE LONE STAR STATE WHEN HE WAS A BABY, AND HE GREW UP IN THE TOWN OF CHESHIRE, CONNECTICUT, WHERE HIS FATHER MANAGED THE TOWN RINK. BY THE TIME HE WAS A TEENAGER, LEETCH WAS A STAR IN TWO ▮▮▮▶

RYAN McDONAGH WAS selected 12th overall by the Montreal Canadiens in 2007, but was traded to the New York Rangers before he got to the NHL. McDonagh is from St. Paul, Minnesota, and attended the University of Wisconsin for three years before making his NHL debut in 2010–11. He doesn't have the same offensive flare that Brian Leetch had, but he shares Leetch's leadership qualities. McDonagh was named captain in 2014, becoming the first Rangers defenseman to wear the "C" since Leetch did so from 1997 to 2000.

MODERN MATCH
RYAN McDONAGH

different sports. In Grade 10, he earned All-State honors in hockey while pitching his local high school baseball team to the state championship. After his senior year at the prestigious Avon Old Farms prep school, Leetch was chosen ninth overall by the New York Rangers in the 1986 NHL Draft.

Leetch didn't join the Rangers right away. In 1986–87, he attended Boston College where his father had also played hockey. The next year, Leetch joined the United States national team and played at the 1988 Calgary Olympics. He joined the Rangers after the Winter Games and picked up an assist in his first NHL contest! Leetch was a strong skater with fantastic offensive instincts. In his first full season with the Rangers in 1988–89, he won the Calder Trophy after scoring 23 goals. That's a rookie record for NHL defensemen that still stands!

Did You Know?

BRIAN LEETCH AND BOBBY ORR ARE THE ONLY PLAYERS IN NHL HISTORY TO WIN THE CALDER, NORRIS AND CONN SMYTHE TROPHIES.

During the next few years, Leetch helped the Rangers grow into champions. In 1991–92, he established career highs with 80 assists and 102 points, joining Bobby Orr, Denis Potvin, Paul Coffey and Al MacInnis as one of only five defensemen in NHL history to top 100 points in a season. Leetch won the Norris Trophy that season, and again in 1996–97. In 1993–94, the Rangers won the Stanley Cup for the first time in 54 years. When they did, Leetch became the first American-born player to win the Conn Smythe Trophy as playoff MVP!

BATTERED BLADES

Brian Leetch wore these skates while starring with the Rangers from 1989 to 1995. They show plenty of wear and tear from six seasons in the NHL. In all, Leetch played 18 seasons in the league before retiring in 2006. He spent 16-plus seasons with the Rangers and holds the franchise record with 741 assists. Leetch was traded to Toronto late in the 2003–04 season. After a lockout wiped out the 2004–05 campaign, he returned to play one final season in the NHL as a member of the Boston Bruins.

FROM THE VAULT

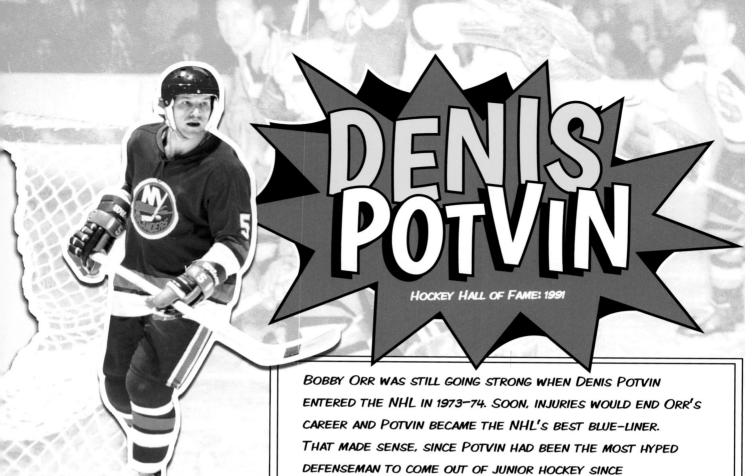

DENIS POTVIN

Hockey Hall of Fame: 1991

BOBBY ORR WAS STILL GOING STRONG WHEN DENIS POTVIN ENTERED THE NHL IN 1973-74. SOON, INJURIES WOULD END ORR'S CAREER AND POTVIN BECAME THE NHL'S BEST BLUE-LINER. THAT MADE SENSE, SINCE POTVIN HAD BEEN THE MOST HYPED DEFENSEMAN TO COME OUT OF JUNIOR HOCKEY SINCE BOBBY ORR. ▐▐▐➤

WHEN AARON EKBLAD was 14 years old, he helped his minor midget team, filled mostly with kids a year or two older, win an Ontario championship. And like Denis Potvin, Ekblad was given special permission to play junior hockey before he reached the minimum age requirement, starring with the Barrie Colts of the Ontario Hockey League (OHL) at 15 years old! In 2014, the Florida Panthers made Ekblad the first overall pick in the NHL Draft and he cracked the lineup right away as an 18-year-old. And just like Potvin years before him, Ekblad was named NHL rookie of the year.

MODERN MATCH
AARON EKBLAD

Like Orr, Potvin began his junior career when he was only 14 years old. During the early 1970s, a player had to be 20 years old to enter the NHL, not 18. That meant Potvin spent five full seasons playing junior hockey. In his final Ontario Hockey League season of 1972–73, Potvin shattered Orr's defenseman record of 94 points by collecting 123 points! The New York Islanders were the worst team in the NHL that season, which gave them the top choice in the 1973 Draft. To no one's surprise, they picked Potvin.

Did You Know?

DENIS POTVIN WON THE NORRIS TROPHY THREE TIMES IN HIS CAREER AND FINISHED SECOND IN VOTING TWICE.

Potvin's older brother Jean played with the Islanders too, and that made it easier for Denis to break into the NHL. He won the Calder Trophy as rookie of the year and soon helped make the Islanders one of the league's best teams. When Potvin was named team captain in 1979–80, he led the Islanders to their first of four straight Stanley Cup wins!

Potvin was strong and sturdy on the ice. He was a tough player who delivered hard hits, but he was just as dangerous in the other team's zone. In 1978–79, Potvin joined Orr as the second defenseman to score 100 points in a season. Potvin was the first defenseman in NHL history to score 300 career goals and also the first to reach 1,000 points. He topped 30 goals on three occasions and had six other seasons with 20 goals or more.

Blast FROM THE Past — HARVEY PULFORD (HHOF: 1945)

There has been a long tradition of hockey excellence in Ottawa, Ontario. In the early 1900s, the Ottawa "Silver Seven" were the game's best team and Harvey Pulford was the team's best defenseman. Pulford played many sports, including lacrosse, football and rowing. In hockey, he was a hardnosed defenseman, who, like Denis Potvin, was unafraid to deliver a punishing check in order to take care of business in his own end. Pulford starred for Ottawa from 1893 to 1908 and helped his team win the Stanley Cup in 1903, 1904, 1905 and 1906!

AL MacINNIS

HOCKEY HALL OF FAME: 2007

AL MacINNIS HAD A BIG SHOT. HE GREW UP IN A FISHING VILLAGE IN NOVA SCOTIA, WHERE HIS FATHER RAN THE LOCAL HOCKEY RINK. MacINNIS USED TO HANG AROUND, COLLECTING PUCKS THAT WENT OVER THE BOARDS. IN SUMMER, HE SPENT HOURS SHOOTING THOSE PUCKS AGAINST HIS FATHER'S BARN. LITTLE DID HE KNOW HE WAS PERFECTING ▐▐▶

HOCKEY HALL OF FAME: 1972

Bernie GEOFFRION

MASTER BLASTER

Like Al MacInnis, Bernie Geoffrion was known for his powerful slap shot. In fact, he was so well known for it that he was nicknamed "Boom Boom." The first boom was from the sound of his stick hitting the puck; the second was the puck hitting the boards. Geoffrion said he invented the shot as a boy in the 1930s, but Bun Cook of the New York Rangers was already using a similar shot. People back then usually called it a golf shot. In 1960–61, Boom Boom became the second player in NHL history to score 50 goals in a single season!

one of the greatest slap shots in hockey history!

The Calgary Flames chose MacInnis in the first round of the 1981 NHL Draft. The team knew they had something special, but they didn't rush him. MacInnis spent most of the next two years playing junior hockey with the Kitchener Rangers. In 1982–83, he was named the best defenseman in the Ontario Hockey League. When he finally made it to Calgary for good midway through the 1983–84 season, MacInnis was ready. Soon, the Flames were one of the best teams in the NHL and MacInnis was one of the league's top defensemen.

MacInnis was solid in front of his own net, but it was his blistering slap shot that had people's attention, especially the terrified goalies on opposing teams! When Calgary won the Stanley Cup in 1989, MacInnis led all playoff performers in scoring. He was the first defenseman to do that in 11 years, and he became just the fourth defenseman in NHL history to win the Conn Smythe Trophy as playoff MVP. During the 1990–91 season, MacInnis joined Bobby Orr, Denis Potvin and Paul Coffey as the fourth defenseman in NHL history to top 100 points in a single season! After 13 years in Calgary, MacInnis was traded to St. Louis in 1994. He played 10 more years with the Blues and won the Norris Trophy with them in 1998–99.

Did You Know?

USING AN OLD-FASHIONED WOODEN STICK, AL MACINNIS WON THE HARDEST SHOT COMPETITION AT THE NHL ALL-STAR GAME SEVEN TIMES.

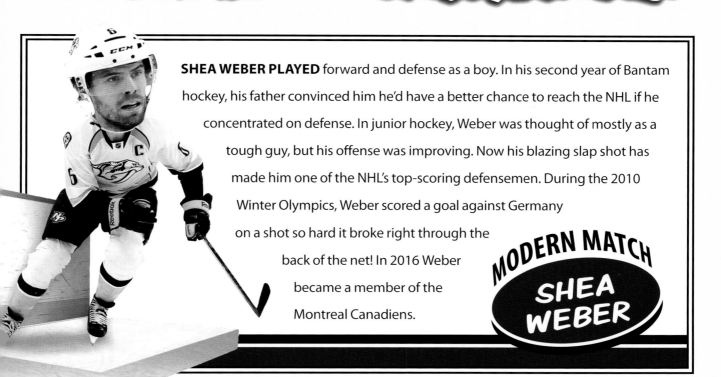

SHEA WEBER PLAYED forward and defense as a boy. In his second year of Bantam hockey, his father convinced him he'd have a better chance to reach the NHL if he concentrated on defense. In junior hockey, Weber was thought of mostly as a tough guy, but his offense was improving. Now his blazing slap shot has made him one of the NHL's top-scoring defensemen. During the 2010 Winter Olympics, Weber scored a goal against Germany on a shot so hard it broke right through the back of the net! In 2016 Weber became a member of the Montreal Canadiens.

MODERN MATCH

SHEA WEBER

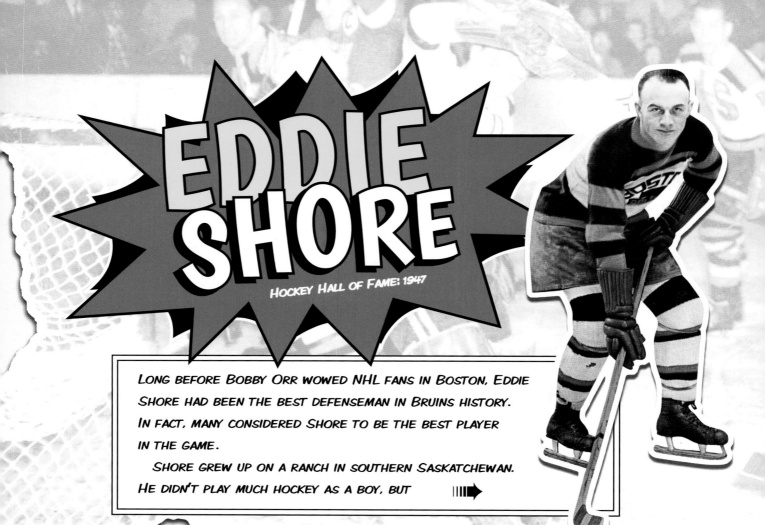

EDDIE SHORE

HOCKEY HALL OF FAME: 1947

LONG BEFORE BOBBY ORR WOWED NHL FANS IN BOSTON, EDDIE SHORE HAD BEEN THE BEST DEFENSEMAN IN BRUINS HISTORY. IN FACT, MANY CONSIDERED SHORE TO BE THE BEST PLAYER IN THE GAME.

SHORE GREW UP ON A RANCH IN SOUTHERN SASKATCHEWAN. HE DIDN'T PLAY MUCH HOCKEY AS A BOY, BUT ▐▐▐▶

AT 6-FOOT-9 (206 cm), Zdeno Chara is the tallest player in NHL history! He broke into the NHL with the New York Islanders in 1997–98 and later became a star with Ottawa. Since signing with Boston in 2006–07, Chara has gotten even better. He won the Norris Trophy for the first time in 2008–09 and captained Boston to the Stanley Cup in 2011. Chara won the hardest shot competition at the NHL All-Star Game five times in a row between 2007 and 2012. His slap shot has regularly been clocked at over 100 miles per hour (160 kph)!

MODERN MATCH

ZDENO CHARA

his years of hard work with the horses on the ranch made him tough and strong. "It helped me build the [body] I needed to play 19 years of professional hockey," Shore once said. When he joined Boston in 1926–27, the Bruins were in just their third season in the NHL. They'd struggled during their first two years, but Shore helped turn them into the best team in the league. The Bruins won the Stanley Cup for the first time in 1929, and Shore was still starring with the team when they won it again in 1939. He also led the Bruins to the best record in the regular season six times!

Shore skated with long strides that carried him up the ice with blazing speed. His strength made it hard to knock him off the puck, and his nasty temper meant opponents had to pay the price if they did. Shore usually ranked among the top-scoring defensemen in the NHL each season, but he was always high among the penalty leaders too. Still, he was clearly the best defenseman in the league. There was no Norris Trophy when Shore played, but when the NHL began naming its year-end All-Star Teams in 1930–31, Shore was named to the First Team seven times in nine years. He's also the only defenseman in NHL history to win the Hart Trophy as league MVP four times.

Did You Know?

SINCE 1959, THE OUTSTANDING DEFENSEMAN IN THE AMERICAN HOCKEY LEAGUE HAS RECEIVED THE EDDIE SHORE PLAQUE.

FROM THE VAULT

SHORE'S LEATHER LID

Eddie Shore's legendary temper once put him in the middle of one of hockey's darkest moments. During a rough game between the Bruins and the Maple Leafs on December 12, 1933, Shore hit Toronto's Ace Bailey from behind. Bailey fell on his head and fractured his skull. For a while, it seemed that Bailey might die from his injuries. He eventually recovered, but never played hockey again. Barely anyone in hockey wore helmets then, but after the Bailey incident, several Boston players began to do so. Eddie Shore wore this leather helmet during the mid-1930s.

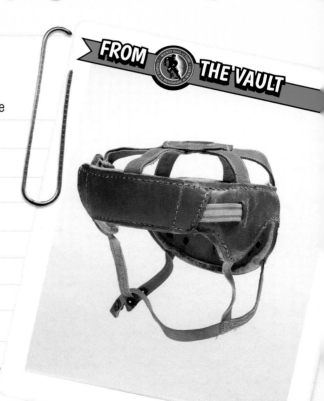

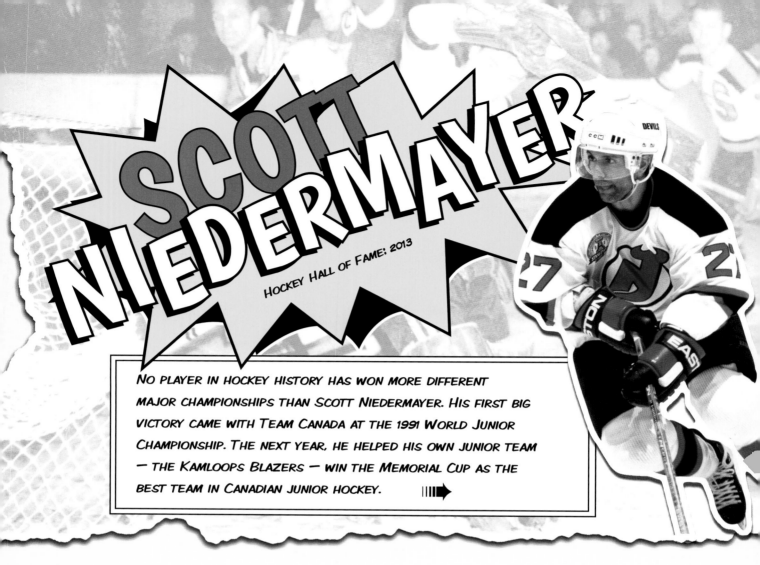

SCOTT NIEDERMAYER

Hockey Hall of Fame: 2013

No player in hockey history has won more different major championships than Scott Niedermayer. His first big victory came with Team Canada at the 1991 World Junior Championship. The next year, he helped his own junior team — the Kamloops Blazers — win the Memorial Cup as the best team in Canadian junior hockey. ▌▌▌▶

CYCLONE TAYLOR (HHOF: 1947) Blast FROM THE Past

Cyclone Taylor never played in the NHL, but he's still one of the biggest stars in hockey history. Taylor became famous as a defenseman with the Ottawa Senators in 1907. His real name was Fred, but people called him Cyclone because of his whirlwind speed. He loved to rush the puck, but was always fast enough to get back and help his goalie. Taylor played forward and the old-time position of rover when he joined the Vancouver Millionaires of the Pacific Coast Hockey Association (PCHA) in 1912. There he won five PCHA scoring titles!

Niedermayer later won the Stanley Cup four times during his 18-year NHL career. In 2004 he helped Canada win gold twice — once at the World Championships and again at the World Cup of Hockey! He also earned Olympic gold medals in 2002 and 2010.

Niedermayer was born in Edmonton, Alberta, but grew up in Cranbrook, British Columbia. In addition to playing hockey as a boy, he took figure skating lessons when he was seven. Those lessons taught him balance and helped him develop the strong stride that made him one of the fastest skaters in the NHL. In fact, Niedermayer was so smooth on his skates that he sometimes made the game look too easy. Early in his career, people wondered if the slick-skating Niedermayer was willing to compete hard enough to become an NHL star. He quickly proved to be a great team player and a hard worker.

Niedermayer became a regular with the New Jersey Devils in 1992–93. Soon, with goalie Martin Brodeur and fellow defenseman Scott Stevens, the Devils became one of the best teams in the NHL. Niedermayer won the Stanley Cup with New Jersey in 1995, 2000 and 2003. He also won the Norris Trophy in 2003–04. Niedermayer joined the Anaheim Ducks in 2005–06. The Devils beat the Ducks for the Stanley Cup in 2003, but with Niedermayer as their captain, Anaheim won the Stanley Cup in 2007. Niedermayer earned the Conn Smythe Trophy as playoff MVP.

Did You Know?

SCOTT NIEDERMAYER WON THE STANLEY CUP PLAYING AGAINST HIS BROTHER ROB'S TEAM IN 2003 AND THEN WON IT WITH HIM WHEN THEY PLAYED TOGETHER IN 2007.

MODERN MATCH
DUNCAN KEITH

HE MAY NOT skate like Scott Niedermayer, but Duncan Keith of the Chicago Blackhawks is also a strong two-way defenseman. He's known for his offensive skill and his shutdown abilities. Keith started as a forward in minor hockey, but played defense in junior. He joined the Blackhawks in 2005–06 and has won the Stanley Cup with Chicago in 2010, 2013 and 2015! In 2010, he was also a teammate of Scott Niedermayer when Team Canada won the Olympic gold. Keith won his second Olympic gold medal in 2014. In 2015 he was named MVP of the NHL playoffs!

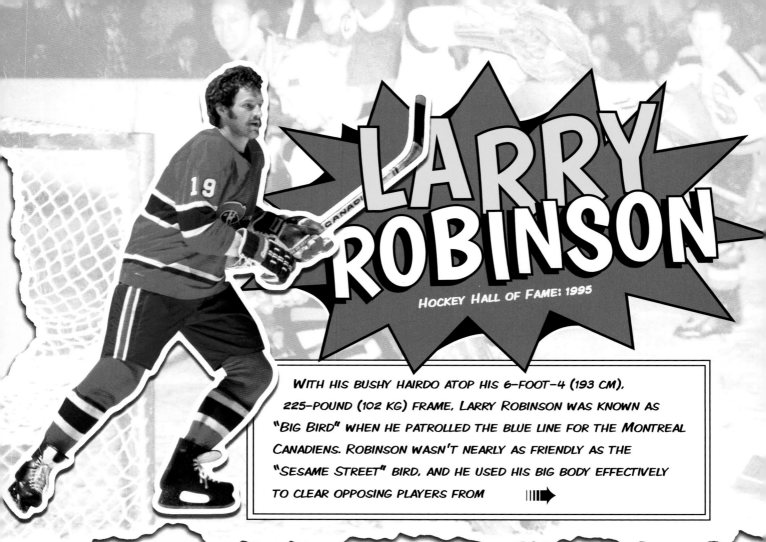

LARRY ROBINSON

Hockey Hall of Fame: 1995

With his bushy hairdo atop his 6-foot-4 (193 cm), 225-pound (102 kg) frame, Larry Robinson was known as "Big Bird" when he patrolled the blue line for the Montreal Canadiens. Robinson wasn't nearly as friendly as the "Sesame Street" bird, and he used his big body effectively to clear opposing players from ▐▐▶

Powerful Pairs

Serge Savard (HHOF: 1986)	Guy Lapointe (HHOF: 1993)

During the 1970s, Larry Robinson was part of a defensive unit in Montreal known as "The Big Three." The other two players were Serge Savard and Guy Lapointe. Savard, a veteran who became famous for the "spinorama," had plenty of offensive skill, but he developed a stay-at-home style that let Robinson take more chances. Lapointe may have had the most offensive talent of The Big Three. Picking his spots to pinch in and aid the attack, Lapointe topped 20 goals three different times.

the front of his net. His big, booming slap shot also made him dangerous in the offensive zone.

Robinson didn't play defense until he got to junior hockey, and he only did then because his team didn't have enough defensemen. When the Canadiens drafted him in 1971, they decided to keep Robinson at his new position, and sent him to the minors to get more experience. He got his first shot with Montreal in 1972–73, and he took a regular shift with the Canadiens for the rest of the season. Montreal decided not to play him at the start of the playoffs that year, but he worked his way back in and helped the team win the Stanley Cup. Later Robinson helped Montreal win the Cup four years in a row! He also won the Norris Trophy twice, and was named the MVP of the playoffs in 1978. Arguably, the Canadiens

Did You Know?

LARRY ROBINSON WAS THE FIRST NHL PLAYER TO PLAY 200 PLAYOFF GAMES AND NOW RANKS EIGHTH ALL-TIME WITH 227 PLAYOFF GAMES.

of the late 1970s were the greatest team in hockey history. Even so, Robinson's best season in Montreal may have been in 1985–86, when the Canadiens were much weaker. That year he had 19 goals and 63 assists for a career-high 82 points, and Montreal was a surprise winner of the Stanley Cup. It was Robinson's sixth NHL championship!

Robinson spent 17 seasons in Montreal and three in Los Angeles. Later, as a coach with New Jersey, he won the Stanley Cup three more times.

THE LOS ANGELES Kings chose Drew Doughty second overall at the 2008 NHL Draft. Though he'd been a star in junior hockey with the Guelph Storm, Doughty was still only 18 and not a lot of people figured he'd make the Los Angeles lineup. He worked hard at training camp, though, and secured a spot on the team. He's been among the best defensemen in the NHL ever since. It'll be tough to match Larry Robinson's six Stanley Cup wins, but Doughty has already won the Cup twice with the Kings, in 2012 and 2014. In 2016, Doughty was awarded his first Norris Trophy.

MODERN MATCH
DREW DOUGHTY

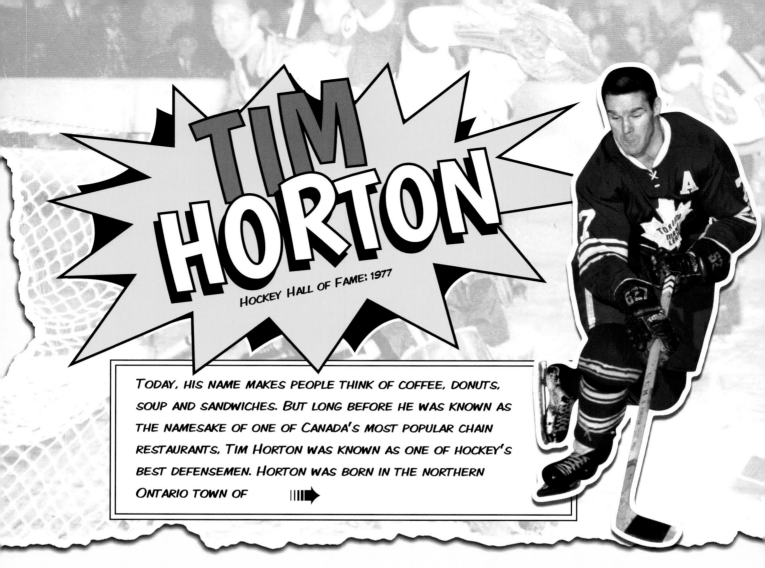

TIM HORTON
HOCKEY HALL OF FAME: 1977

Today, his name makes people think of coffee, donuts, soup and sandwiches. But long before he was known as the namesake of one of Canada's most popular chain restaurants, Tim Horton was known as one of hockey's best defensemen. Horton was born in the northern Ontario town of ▐▐▐▶

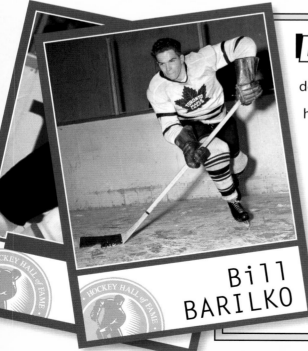

Bill
BARILKO

LEAF LEGENDS

Tim Horton was the tough defenseman Toronto needed to replace a lost legend. Bill Barilko had scored the Stanley Cup-winning goal for the Maple Leafs in 1951, but he disappeared in a plane crash late that summer. Horton started fulltime with the Leafs in 1952. Bariklo had only been with the Leafs for five seasons, yet he'd helped them win the Stanley Cup four times! Known as "Bashing Bill" for his powerful body checks, Barilko was one of the hardest hitters in hockey. After his death, the Leafs didn't win the Stanley Cup again until 1962 — the same year Barilko's remains were finally discovered.

Cochrane and later played hockey around nearby Timmins. His real name was Miles Gilbert Horton, but his mother always called him Tim. By the time he was 17, Horton had attracted the attention of the Toronto Maple Leafs. They arranged for him to go to St. Michael's College in Toronto so he could attend school and play hockey. Horton turned pro with the Maple Leafs in 1949, but he wasn't a full-time member of the club until 1952–53. A badly broken leg suffered late in the 1954–55 season slowed him down for the next few years, but by the early 1960s, the Maple Leafs were the best team in hockey and Horton was their best defenseman. With Horton on the blue line, Toronto won the Stanley Cup in 1962, 1963, 1964 and 1967! Coach Punch Imlach would later say that the tough defenseman was more important to those Cup-winning teams than any other player.

Horton was known as the strongest man in the NHL. He could deliver crushing body checks, but he usually used his incredible strength to stop fights, rather than start them. When trouble began, Horton would restrain a player in a powerful grip that became known as the "Horton Bear Hug." His talent and strength kept people in line, and his smooth skating made him an effective player at both ends of the ice. Sadly, Tim Horton was killed in a car accident in 1974 while a member of the Buffalo Sabres.

Did You Know?

TIM HORTON OPENED HIS FIRST RESTAURANT IN HAMILTON, ONTARIO, IN 1964. TODAY, THERE ARE MORE THAN 3,000 TIM HORTONS ACROSS CANADA.

Blast FROM THE Past

HAP DAY (HHOF: 1961)

Clarence Day was so cheerful his friends called him "Happy." Soon, that was shortened to "Hap," and the nickname stuck. Hap Day was originally a defenseman, but when he started in the NHL with the Toronto St. Pats in 1924 they played him at left wing. By the time the team became the Maple Leafs in 1926–27, Day was back on defense. He was a natural-born leader who served as team captain from 1927–28 to 1936–37. Day won the Stanley Cup as a player in 1932 and later coached the Maple Leafs to five more championships in the 1940s!

DOUG HARVEY

HOCKEY HALL OF FAME: 1973

WHENEVER PEOPLE TALK ABOUT THE BEST DEFENSEMEN IN HOCKEY HISTORY, DOUG HARVEY'S NAME IS NEAR THE TOP OF THE LIST. NO ONE IN THE 1950S COULD TAKE CARE OF BUSINESS IN HIS OWN END BETTER THAN HARVEY, AND NO DEFENSEMAN IN THE NHL COULD PASS THE PUCK TO HIS FORWARDS AS WELL AS HE DID. HARVEY WAS SO GOOD WITH THE PUCK THAT ||||➤

FROM THE VAULT

LAST HURRAH

Doug Harvey's NHL career seemed to be over when the New York Rangers decided he was too old for them during the 1963–64 season. He played in the minor leagues for the next few years and when the St. Louis Blues joined the NHL as a new expansion team in 1967–68, they signed Harvey as a player-coach for their farm team. Harvey was called up to the NHL when St. Louis made the playoffs, and he helped the Blues reach the Stanley Cup Final. He wore this jersey for the Blues against his old team, the Montreal Canadiens.

he controlled the way everyone on the ice played. When he slowed down to survey the situation and look for an opening, everyone else slowed down too. When he sped up again, every player on the ice moved faster. Harvey was the best defenseman on the best team in the NHL, helping the Montreal Canadiens win the Stanley Cup in 1953 and for a record five years in a row from 1956 to 1960!

Great as he was at hockey, Harvey also starred at football and baseball. He was so good at baseball that the Boston Braves of the National League invited him to spring training in 1950. Harvey couldn't go though, as he was a little busy playing in the NHL playoffs with Montreal at the time!

Harvey joined the Canadiens in 1947–48. It took him a little while to adjust to the NHL, but by 1951–52 he was a First-Team

Did You Know?

AMONG DEFENSEMEN, ONLY RAYMOND BOURQUE (19) AND NICKLAS LIDSTROM (12) HAVE BEEN SELECTED AS NHL ALL-STARS MORE TIMES THAN DOUG HARVEY.

All-Star. Harvey was an All-Star for 11 straight seasons, including 10 selections to the First Team. When the NHL began awarding the Norris Trophy in 1954, Harvey won it six times in the first eight years! He won it for a seventh time in 1961–62. He was a member of the New York Rangers that season, serving as a star player and as the team's head coach. In all, Harvey played 20 NHL seasons and retired in 1969 at the age of 44.

MODERN MATCH

P.K. SUBBAN

SIX DIFFERENT DEFENSEMEN have won the Norris Trophy while playing for the Montreal Canadiens, more than any other team in the NHL. The most recent member of this record-setting club is Pernell Karl Subban. Better known as P.K. Subban, he won the Norris Trophy in 2012–13. Subban is a great skater with a hard shot. He can lead his team on the power play and shut down opponents in his own end, something his new team, the Nashville Predators, will appreciate. Fans sometimes get nervous when he takes chances with the puck, but Subban is one of the most exciting young defensemen in the NHL.

SCOTT STEVENS

HOCKEY HALL OF FAME: 2007

FOR SOMEONE WHO PLAYED AS ROUGH AS HE DID, SCOTT STEVENS WAS REMARKABLY DURABLE. HE PLAYED 22 SEASONS IN THE NHL AND RANKS SEVENTH ALL-TIME IN GAMES PLAYED WITH 1,635. CHRIS CHELIOS IS THE ONLY DEFENSEMAN IN NHL HISTORY TO HAVE PLAYED MORE GAMES THAN HE DID. STEVENS WAS ONE OF THE HARDEST ▐▐▐▶

SPRAGUE CLEGHORN (HHOF: 1958) Blast FROM THE Past

Sprague Cleghorn played seven seasons of pro hockey, much of it with the Montreal Wanderers, in the years before the NHL was formed. He later starred in the NHL until 1927–28, often playing with his brother Odie. Sprague is considered to be one of the toughest players of all-time. In fact, many oldtimers thought he was the dirtiest player they ever faced! Still, there was no denying that Cleghorn had talent. He won the Stanley Cup with Ottawa in 1920 and 1921 and was captain of the Montreal Canadiens when they won it in 1924.

hitters in hockey history. Sometimes, he was accused of playing dirty, but mostly he was admired for his tough, physical skill.

Stevens played just one full season of junior hockey. He was a teammate of future Hall of Famer Al MacInnis with the Kitchener Rangers in 1981–82 and helped that team win the Memorial Cup. Stevens was then selected fifth overall by the Washington Capitals in the 1982 NHL Draft and made the team right away. In Washington, Stevens played with two other future Hall of Fame defensemen: Rod Langway and Larry Murphy. During the first half of his career, Stevens picked up plenty of points. He scored a career-high 21 goals for Washington in 1984–85 and had 60-plus assists three times. In 1993–94 he had a career-best 78 points for the New Jersey Devils.

Over his years in New Jersey, Stevens

concentrated more on his hard-hitting defensive skills and the Devils became the NHL's toughest team to score against. He knew the Norris Trophy usually went to a defenseman with a lot of points, but he didn't mind that focusing on stopping scorers would limit his chances at winning the trophy. Stevens was captain of the Devils from 1992–93 until his final season of 2002–03 and he led the team to three Stanley Cup wins. Stevens never did win the Norris Trophy, but he won the Conn Smythe Trophy as playoff MVP in 2000.

DUSTIN BYFUGLIEN (pronounced "Bufflin") is built more like a football linebacker than a hockey player. Though he keeps his game pretty clean, just the sight of the 6-foot-5 (196 cm), 265-pound (120 kg) defenseman can be intimidating! Byfuglien played defense in junior hockey and joined the Chicago Blackhawks as a defenseman in 2005–06. In 2007–08, Chicago moved him to right wing to take advantage of his size in front of the other team's net. Byfuglien helped Chicago win the Stanley Cup in 2010. Then he was traded to the Winnipeg Jets, where once again he is an imposing force on the blue line.

MODERN MATCH

DUSTIN BYFUGLIEN

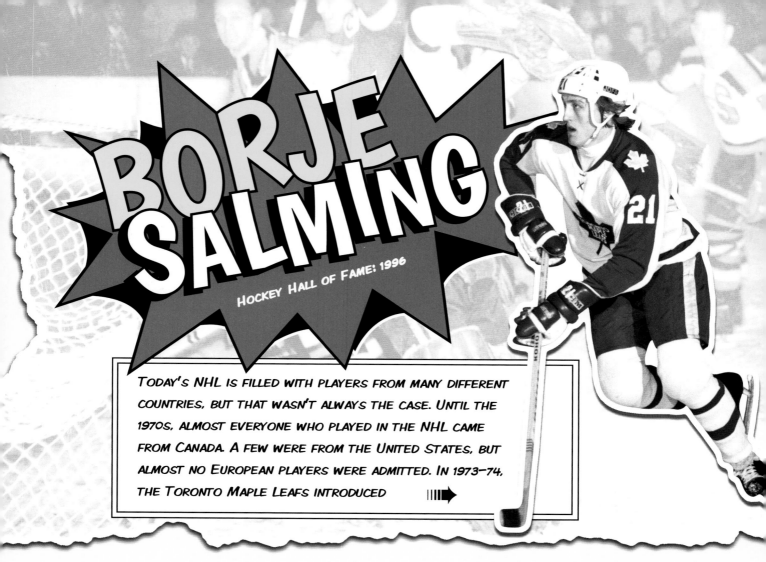

BORJE SALMING

Hockey Hall of Fame: 1996

Today's NHL is filled with players from many different countries, but that wasn't always the case. Until the 1970s, almost everyone who played in the NHL came from Canada. A few were from the United States, but almost no European players were admitted. In 1973–74, the Toronto Maple Leafs introduced

RED HORNER (HHOF: 1965)   Blast FROM THE Past

Unlike Salming, nobody ever had to wonder if Red Horner was tough enough to play in the NHL. He was a solid defenseman who starred for 12 seasons with the Toronto Maple Leafs, from 1928 to 1940. For much of that time, Horner was known as the "Bad Boy of Hockey," as he led the NHL in penalty minutes seven of his last eight seasons. But Horner was no mere goon. He helped the Leafs finish first in their division four times and he won the Stanley Cup with Toronto in 1932. He was also captain of the Leafs from 1938 until he retired.

a 22-year-old defenseman from Sweden. Borje Salming was not the first European player to make it to the NHL, but he was the first to become a star. His success opened the door for every European player that has followed.

It was almost an accident that Salming made it to the NHL. The Maple Leafs were actually looking at another Swedish player when they noticed Salming. Toronto signed Salming and fellow Swede Inge Hammarstrom. There was not much body contact in Swedish hockey, and people wondered if Salming would be tough enough for the NHL. Players on other teams called him "chicken" and tried to scare him with rough play. Salming never let the bullies get him down and he soon earned everyone's respect.

Salming kept himself in great shape and often played more than half the game. He was a fearless shot-blocker, which was rare back then because protective gear was so much smaller than it is today. By his second season of 1974–75, he was comfortable enough in the NHL to unleash his offensive skill. He became known for his dazzling zigzag rushes and slick passes. He didn't have a big slap shot, but his wrist shot was dangerous. Salming finished his NHL career with the Detroit Red Wings in 1989–90, but remains one of the most popular Maple Leafs of all time. He never won the Norris Trophy as the NHL's best defenseman, but finished second in voting twice.

Did You Know?

IN THE 16 SEASONS HE SPENT IN TORONTO, BORJE SALMING BECAME THE MAPLE LEAFS' ALL-TIME LEADER WITH 620 ASSISTS.

LIKE SALMING, ERIK Karlsson is a powerful skater who can fly across the ice. He's got a booming slap shot too! When he was only 17 years old, Karlsson had already reached the top league in Sweden. Later that year, Ottawa selected him in the first round of the 2008 NHL Draft. He joined the Senators in 2009–10. Karlsson led all NHL defensemen with 78 points in 2011–12 and won the Norris Trophy that season. He'd barely turned 22 when the award was announced, making him the youngest Norris Trophy winner since Bobby Orr in 1968.

MODERN MATCH
ERIK KARLSSON

RAYMOND BOURQUE

HOCKEY HALL OF FAME: 2004

RAYMOND BOURQUE BROKE INTO THE NHL IN 1979-80, THE SAME YEAR AS WAYNE GRETZKY. BOURQUE WAS THE WINNER OF THE CALDER TROPHY AS ROOKIE OF THE YEAR THAT SEASON. THE NHL DECIDED GRETZKY COULDN'T WIN THE AWARD BECAUSE HE PLAYED PROFESSIONALLY IN THE WORLD HOCKEY ASSOCIATION THE YEAR BEFORE. EVEN SO, BOURQUE ▐▐▐▶

RYAN SUTER IS part of a famous American hockey family. His father, Bob Suter, won a gold medal with the 1980 U.S. Olympic team. His uncle, Gary Suter, had a 17-year career in the NHL. Ryan began his NHL career with Nashville in 2005. He quickly became a star defenseman, but he got even better with Minnesota. With the Wild in 2012–13, Suter had more time on ice than any other player in the NHL. He was named the league's best defenseman by *The Hockey News* and finished second in voting for the Norris Trophy behind Montreal's P.K. Subban.

MODERN MATCH

RYAN SUTER

had an amazing season! His 65 points that year set a record for rookie defensemen. Not only did Bourque win the Calder Trophy, he was also named a First-Team All-Star. It was the first time in NHL history that anyone but a goalie had won both awards in one year. Bourque went on to earn 13 selections to the First All-Star Team during his 22-year career. That's the most by anyone who's ever played in the NHL!

Bourque played with a calm style that made things look easy. He was a smooth, effortless skater, and he

kept himself in excellent shape, which allowed him to get plenty of ice time. Even late in his career, Bourque often played more than 30 minutes per game! He had plenty of offensive skill, but he was truly a two-way talent. He could play a strong, physical game in his own end of the rink, and also make passes with great finesse to set up his teammates. Bourque reached a career high with 31 goals in 1983–84 and scored 20 goals or more eight other times. The only time he failed to score at least 10 goals was in his final NHL season, when he was 40 years old.

When Bourque retired in 2001, he'd become the all-time leader among NHL defensemen with 410 goals and 1,169 assists for 1,579 points. He'd also won the Norris Trophy five times.

Did You Know?

RAYMOND BOURQUE WAS CAPTAIN OF THE BOSTON BRUINS FOR A TEAM-RECORD 12 YEARS FROM 1988 TO 2000.

CUP-WINNING THREADS

Raymond Bourque played 20 full seasons for the Boston Bruins. He was one of the greatest players in the NHL, but he'd never won the Stanley Cup. Late in the 1999–2000 season, Bourque was traded to Colorado, one of the top teams in the NHL at that time. In 2000–01, the Avalanche plotted mission 16W — 16 wins being the amount of playoff victories a team needed to claim the Stanley Cup. When they completed the mission, Bourque was the first player to raise the Cup over his head. Bourque wore this jersey during the second period of Game 7 in the 2001 Stanley Cup Final.

FROM THE VAULT

CHRIS PRONGER

Hockey Hall of Fame: 2015

Standing 6-foot-6 (198 cm) and weighing 220 pounds (99 kg), Chris Pronger was a blond-haired giant on the blue line for 18 seasons in the NHL from 1993–94 to 2011–12. He loved to use his big body to deliver punishing checks, but Pronger also often ranked among the NHL's top-scoring defensemen. ▐▐▐▶

HART OF THE MATTER:
Defensemen and the MVP Award

Chris Pronger is one of only eight defensemen in NHL history who have won the Hart Trophy. The first to do it was Herb Gardiner of the Montreal Canadiens in 1926–27. Babe Siebert won it with Montreal in 1936–37; Ebbie Goodfellow won it with Detroit in 1939–40; and Babe Pratt won in with Toronto in 1943–44. Eddie Shore won the Hart four times in the 1930s and Bobby Orr won it three times in the 1970s. Those players are all in the Hockey Hall of Fame. The only non-Hall of Fame defenseman to win the Hart is Tom Anderson of the Brooklyn Americans in 1941–42.

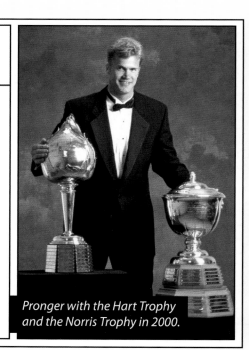

Pronger with the Hart Trophy and the Norris Trophy in 2000.

Pronger was drafted second overall in 1993 and played 81 games for the Hartford Whalers that season. He totaled 30 points and was named to the NHL's All-Rookie Team. But after a poor second season in Hartford, the Whalers traded him to the St. Louis Blues for future Hall of Famer Brendan Shanahan. There was a lot of pressure on Pronger to be a top player in St. Louis, and he was up to the task. On a defense corps that also included Al MacInnis, Pronger became one of the best in the game. He was named captain of the Blues in 1997–98 and led the NHL in plus/minus that season at plus-47. Two years later, Pronger was even better. He established career highs in 1999–2000 with 14 goals, 48 assists, 62 points, and a plus/minus of plus-52 to lead the league again. The Blues set a club record with 114 points that season and finished first overall in the NHL standings for the first time in team history. Not only did Pronger win the Norris Trophy, he became the first defenseman since Bobby Orr in 1971–72 to win the Hart Trophy as NHL MVP!

Pronger was traded to Edmonton in 2005–06 and led the Oilers to the Stanley Cup Final that season. A year later, playing with Scott Niedermayer in Anaheim, Pronger helped the Ducks win their first Stanley Cup. Later, he would help the Philadelphia Flyers reach the Cup Final in 2010.

Did You Know?

ON JUNE 5, 2006, CHRIS PRONGER BECAME THE FIRST NHL PLAYER IN HISTORY TO SCORE A GOAL ON A PENALTY SHOT DURING A STANLEY CUP FINAL.

Blast from the Past   ROD LANGWAY

The main job of any defenseman is to help stop the other team from scoring. Still, the defensemen who attract the most attention are the ones who can help the offense too. So, it's rare when a shutdown defenseman is considered among the greats of the game. Rod Langway scored just three goals for the Washington Capitals in 1982–83 and yet he won the Norris Trophy. No other winner of the award has ever scored fewer goals! Langway won the Norris Trophy again in 1983–84 and almost beat Wayne Gretzky as the league MVP, even though he only scored nine goals.

HOCKEY HALL OF FAME: 2002

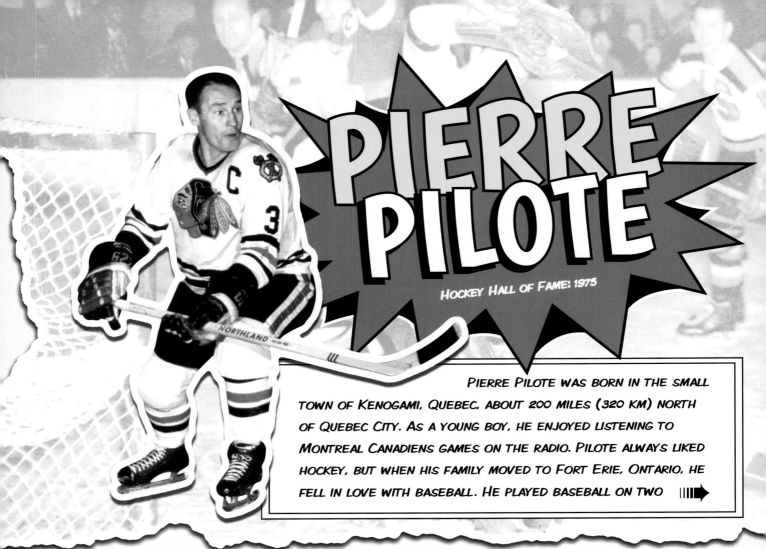

PIERRE PILOTE

HOCKEY HALL OF FAME: 1975

PIERRE PILOTE WAS BORN IN THE SMALL TOWN OF KENOGAMI, QUEBEC, ABOUT 200 MILES (320 KM) NORTH OF QUEBEC CITY. AS A YOUNG BOY, HE ENJOYED LISTENING TO MONTREAL CANADIENS GAMES ON THE RADIO. PILOTE ALWAYS LIKED HOCKEY, BUT WHEN HIS FAMILY MOVED TO FORT ERIE, ONTARIO, HE FELL IN LOVE WITH BASEBALL. HE PLAYED BASEBALL ON TWO ▶

JACK STEWART (HHOF: 1964) — Blast FROM THE Past

Jack Stewart was known as the hardest hitting defenseman of his era. Opponents often said he got a big smile on his face when he was about to give a check. Like Pilote, he was rough, and sometimes took a lot of penalties, but most of his hits were clean. Stewart joined the Red Wings in 1938–39 and helped Detroit win the Stanley Cup in 1942–43 and 1949–50. He was traded to Chicago before the 1950–51 season and was immediately named team captain. Stewart suffered two serious injuries while playing in Chicago and retired from the NHL in 1952.

All-Ontario champions and dreamed of making the Majors. Pilote was 16 before he started playing hockey seriously. Soon, he was good enough that NHL teams were interested.

Pilote began playing junior hockey in St. Catharines, near his home in Fort Erie, in 1950. In 1952, he turned pro with the Buffalo Bisons of the American Hockey League. Then, in 1955, the Black Hawks bought the Bisons and made the club their farm team; with the purchase, Chicago was given the rights to the Bisons' players. Before long, Pilote was playing with the Black Hawks. Chicago was the worst team in the league back then, but soon, other players arrived from the farm system. With Pilote, Bobby Hull, Stan Mikita and others, things quickly got better in Chicago.

Pilote was aggressive and often difficult to deal with. When he was younger he would lose his temper and take bad penalties. He became more effective when he learned to control his temper, and his strong play helped Chicago win the Stanley Cup in 1960–61. The next season Pilote was named captain! Pilote was always a strong checker in his own end, but he was also very good at passing the puck. His all-around play was rewarded in 1962–63 when he won the Norris Trophy for the first of three straight seasons. In 1964–65, Pilote had 14 goals and 45 assists for 59 points, which set a new record for defensemen at that time.

MODERN MATCH

BRENT SEABROOK

AT 6-FOOT-3 (190 cm) and 221 pounds (100 kg), Brent Seabrook has a great combination of size, strength and speed. He's solid in his own end and often gets a lot of ice time against the other team's best forwards. Seabrook also has a hard shot from the blue line and is good at passing the puck. Chicago picked Seabrook 14th overall in the 2003 NHL Draft. He joined the Blackhawks in 2005–06 and helped them win the Stanley Cup in 2010. Seabrook scored two big overtime goals during the 2013 playoffs to help Chicago win the Cup again. He won a third Cup with Chicago in 2015.

BRAD PARK

Hockey Hall of Fame: 1988

It was Brad Park's bad luck that his career overlapped Bobby Orr's best years. Many people think Orr is the greatest defenseman in hockey history. Park always seemed to be runner-up; in fact, he never won the Norris Trophy as the league's best defenseman, but was second in voting six times! Like Orr, Park was a strong

Blast from the Past

CHING JOHNSON (HHOF: 1958)

Ching Johnson joined the New York Rangers when they entered the NHL in 1926–27. At 5-foot-11 (180 cm) and 210 pounds (95 kg), he was huge for his era and was one of the game's hardest checkers. His defense partner, Clarence "Taffy" Abel, was even bigger, at 6-foot-1 (185 cm) and 225 pounds (103 kg). It was tough for any forward to get past those two! There was no Norris Trophy back then, but in the first four years that the NHL chose All-Stars, Johnson earned two selections to the First Team and two to the Second.

skater who loved to rush the puck. He was also a smart playmaker with a hard, accurate shot. Defensively, Park would steer opponents away from the middle of the ice and toward the boards. Even when a player seemed to beat him, that player was usually in poor position for a shot on goal.

When Park was playing minor hockey in Toronto, people worried that he was too small to make the NHL. It's true that Park was barely 5-feet tall (152 cm) when he was 15 years old, but he later shot up to 6-feet (183 cm) and 200 pounds (91 kg). In 1966, the New York Rangers made him the second pick in the NHL Draft. When he joined the team in 1968–69, Park finished third in voting for the rookie of the year. In 1969–70, he finished second to Orr for the Norris Trophy and joined the great Boston Bruins blueliner as a First-Team

Did You Know?

WHEN HE RETIRED IN 1985, BRAD PARK'S 683 CAREER ASSISTS WERE THE MOST EVER BY AN NHL DEFENSEMAN.

All-Star. At 21 years old, Park was the youngest Ranger ever to earn that honor. In 1972, he helped the Rangers reach the Stanley Cup Final.

Park was named captain of the Rangers in 1974, but early in the 1975–76 season he was traded to Boston. Knee injuries had practically ended Bobby Orr's career and Park replaced him on the Bruins blue line. Park helped the Bruins reach the finals in 1977 and 1978, but he never won the Stanley Cup.

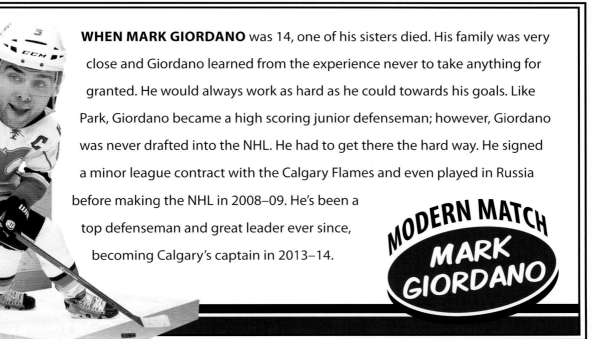

WHEN MARK GIORDANO was 14, one of his sisters died. His family was very close and Giordano learned from the experience never to take anything for granted. He would always work as hard as he could towards his goals. Like Park, Giordano became a high scoring junior defenseman; however, Giordano was never drafted into the NHL. He had to get there the hard way. He signed a minor league contract with the Calgary Flames and even played in Russia before making the NHL in 2008–09. He's been a top defenseman and great leader ever since, becoming Calgary's captain in 2013–14.

MODERN MATCH
MARK GIORDANO

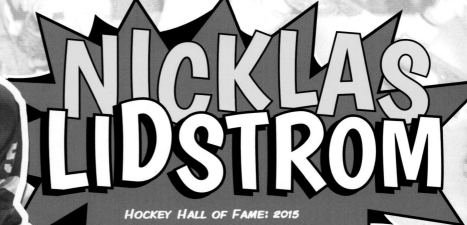

NICKLAS LIDSTROM

Hockey Hall of Fame: 2015

Few players at any position have been as consistently excellent over as long a career as Nicklas Lidstrom. He played 20 seasons in the NHL, all with the Detroit Red Wings, and usually ranked highly among the league leaders in time-on-ice and scoring by a defenseman.

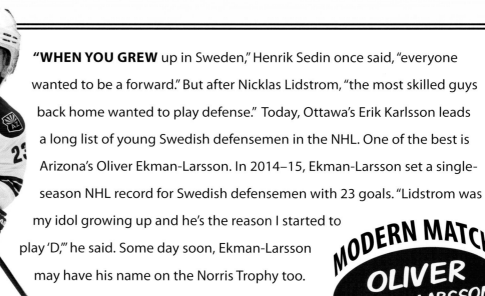

"WHEN YOU GREW up in Sweden," Henrik Sedin once said, "everyone wanted to be a forward." But after Nicklas Lidstrom, "the most skilled guys back home wanted to play defense." Today, Ottawa's Erik Karlsson leads a long list of young Swedish defensemen in the NHL. One of the best is Arizona's Oliver Ekman-Larsson. In 2014–15, Ekman-Larsson set a single-season NHL record for Swedish defensemen with 23 goals. "Lidstrom was my idol growing up and he's the reason I started to play 'D,'" he said. Some day soon, Ekman-Larsson may have his name on the Norris Trophy too.

MODERN MATCH
OLIVER EKMAN-LARSSON

Lidstrom kept himself in great shape, so he rarely missed a game. He wasn't a heavy hitter like some blue line bashers, but he was strong and he was smart. He used good positioning to defend his end of the ice, so he rarely had to take penalties. Lidstrom never won the Lady Byng Trophy — defensemen rarely do — but he finished in the top five in voting 11 times in his career. Five of those times, he finished in second place. Lidstrom did win plenty of awards, though. He earned the Norris Trophy as best defenseman seven times in his career. That ties him with Doug Harvey for the second most Norris Trophy wins in NHL history, one behind Bobby Orr's record of eight. Lidstrom's 10 selections as a First-Team All-Star also tie him with Doug Harvey for the second most by a defenseman, behind Raymond Bourque's record of 13. After winning the Stanley Cup with Detroit in 1997, 1998 and 2002, the native of Sweden became

the first European player to win the Conn Smythe Trophy as the MVP of the playoffs for the 2002 postseason.

Lidstrom succeeded Steve Yzerman as Red Wings captain in 2006–07, and after being named the best European-trained player in NHL history by *The Hockey News* in 2007, he became the first European player to captain his team to the Stanley Cup in 2008. In international hockey, Lidstrom helped Sweden win the World Championship in 1991 before he began his NHL career. He won an Olympic gold medal in 2006.

Did You Know?

NICKLAS LIDSTROM MADE THE PLAYOFFS WITH THE RED WINGS DURING EVERY ONE OF HIS 20 SEASONS.

DETROIT'S 20-YEAR PLAYERS No one in NHL history who has played for only one team has suited up for more games than Nicklas Lidstrom. He played 1,564 games in the regular season, all with Detroit. Second and third on the NHL's list of players who played the most games with one club also spent their entire careers in Detroit. Alex Delvecchio played 1,549 games with the Red Wings in his 24-year career, while Steve Yzerman played 1,514 games over 22 years. The great Gordie Howe actually played 1,687 games for Detroit in 25 years, but he spent his final NHL season with the Hartford Whalers.

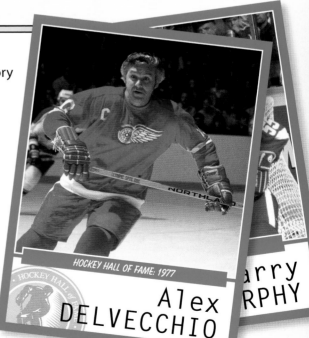

HOCKEY HALL OF FAME: 1977

Alex DELVECCHIO

arry RPHY

CHRIS CHELIOS

Hockey Hall of Fame: 2013

Chris Chelios is a dinosaur! Well, not really, but by the time he retired no defenseman in NHL history had a longer career than him. He played his last NHL game when he was 48 years old! He ranks fifth all-time in games played in the regular season with 1,651. Only Gordie Howe can match the 26 seasons Chelios spent in the NHL. ▐▌▐▌▶

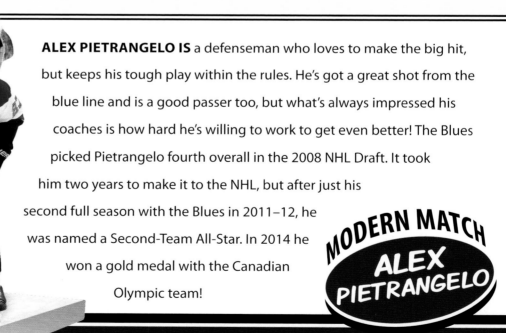

ALEX PIETRANGELO IS a defenseman who loves to make the big hit, but keeps his tough play within the rules. He's got a great shot from the blue line and is a good passer too, but what's always impressed his coaches is how hard he's willing to work to get even better! The Blues picked Pietrangelo fourth overall in the 2008 NHL Draft. It took him two years to make it to the NHL, but after just his second full season with the Blues in 2011–12, he was named a Second-Team All-Star. In 2014 he won a gold medal with the Canadian Olympic team!

MODERN MATCH
ALEX PIETRANGELO

Chelios learned to play hockey in his hometown of Chicago, but it looked like he might have to stop playing when he was 15 and his family moved to California. There were no local teams to play on. Finally, when he was 17, Chelios ventured to Canada and joined the Moose Jaw Canucks in Saskatchewan. He was moved from forward to defense and was good enough that the Montreal Canadiens took him in the second round of the 1981 NHL Draft. In his first full season with the Canadiens in 1984–85, Chelios finished second in voting behind Mario Lemieux for rookie of the year. The next season, he helped the Canadiens win the Stanley Cup. Soon, Chelios was one of the best defensemen in the NHL. He won his first Norris Trophy in 1988–89.

Chelios was traded to Chicago in 1990 and won the Norris Trophy twice with the

Did You Know?

CHRIS CHELIOS REACHED THE PLAYOFFS A RECORD 24 TIMES IN HIS 26-YEAR CAREER AND IS THE NHL ALL-TIME LEADER WITH 266 PLAYOFF GAMES PLAYED.

Blackhawks. He was captain of the team from 1995 until 1999 when he was traded to Detroit. He helped the Red Wings win the Stanley Cup in 2002 and 2008. Chelios never looked fancy on the ice, but he was strong and tough. He was a good offensive defenseman, but it was his hard hits and all-out effort that made him so great. Chelios' secret to playing for so many years was to keep himself in peak physical shape. His workouts even included surfing!

Blast FROM THE Past — BUTCH BOUCHARD

Growing up during The Great Depression, Butch Bouchard couldn't afford to buy skates. He didn't even learn to skate until he was 16, but Bouchard was a great athlete and took to hockey quickly. In 1941, he rode his bicycle 35 miles (50 km) to go to training camp with the Montreal Canadiens! He made the team, and played with them for 15 years. Bouchard helped Montreal win the Stanley Cup four times and was captain of the team from 1948 to 1956. His strong play in his own end allowed defense partner Doug Harvey the freedom to rush with the puck.

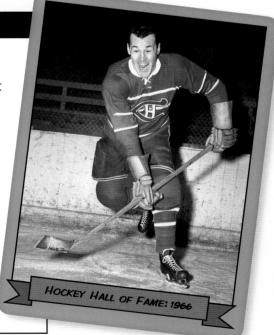

HOCKEY HALL OF FAME: 1966

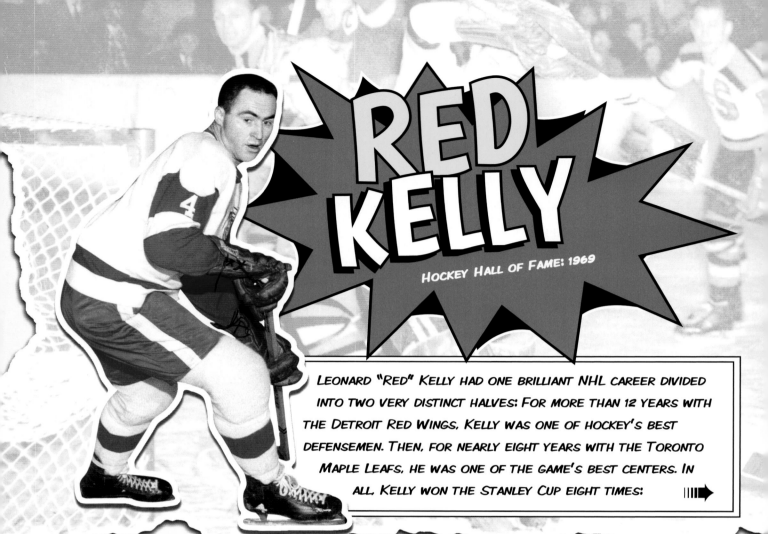

RED KELLY

HOCKEY HALL OF FAME: 1969

LEONARD "RED" KELLY HAD ONE BRILLIANT NHL CAREER DIVIDED INTO TWO VERY DISTINCT HALVES: FOR MORE THAN 12 YEARS WITH THE DETROIT RED WINGS, KELLY WAS ONE OF HOCKEY'S BEST DEFENSEMEN. THEN, FOR NEARLY EIGHT YEARS WITH THE TORONTO MAPLE LEAFS, HE WAS ONE OF THE GAME'S BEST CENTERS. IN ALL, KELLY WON THE STANLEY CUP EIGHT TIMES. ▐▐▐▶

Blast FROM THE Past

DIT CLAPPER (HHOF: 1947)

Like Kelly, Dit Clapper split his time between forward and defense. He was the first person to play 20 seasons in the NHL, and he spent his entire career in Boston. Clapper played right wing when he joined the Bruins in 1927–28. He helped them win the Stanley Cup in 1929 and soon became one of the NHL's top scorers. After 10 seasons at right wing, Boston moved Clapper to defense in 1937–38. A year later, he helped the Bruins win the Stanley Cup again! Clapper was an All-Star twice at right wing and four times as a defenseman.

four times with Detroit and four times with Toronto! His eight Stanley Cup wins are the most ever for someone who never played for the Montreal Canadiens — and they won a lot of Stanley Cups!

Kelly grew up in the small town of Simcoe, Ontario, and he cheered for the Maple Leafs. His favorite player was Toronto defenseman Red Horner, who (like Kelly) was nicknamed for his hair color. Horner, however, was one of the roughest players in NHL history, and when Kelly made the NHL he played a completely different style. Kelly

Did You Know?

RED KELLY WAS THE WINNER OF THE NORRIS TROPHY THE FIRST TIME IT WAS PRESENTED, BACK IN 1953–54.

won the Lady Byng Trophy for sportsmanship four times, which is a rare feat for a defenseman because stopping offensive players often means using rough play, and that leads to penalties. After Kelly won the Byng in 1953–54, it took almost 60 years for another defenseman to win it!

Kelly had hoped to play with the Maple Leafs, but it was the Red Wings that invited him to training camp. He made the team right away in 1947 and built a reputation for playing clean yet strong hockey. He was an effective checker, and his solid skating and puck-moving skills helped Detroit on offense. With other stars such as Gordie Howe, Ted Lindsay and Terry Sawchuk, Detroit quickly became the top team in the NHL. From 1948–49 to 1954–55, the Red Wings finished first in the regular-season standings a record seven years in a row!

VICTORY GARB

Red Kelly wore this jersey for Toronto throughout the 1966–67 season. There were only six teams in the NHL back then. The Chicago Black Hawks were the best team in the NHL that season, but the Maple Leafs shocked them in the opening round of the playoffs. Then, in the finals, Toronto beat Montreal in six games to win the Stanley Cup! Kelly was one of several veterans with Toronto that season. Even though he was 39 years old, the Maple Leafs offered him a new, four-year contract, but Kelly decided to retire while he was on top.

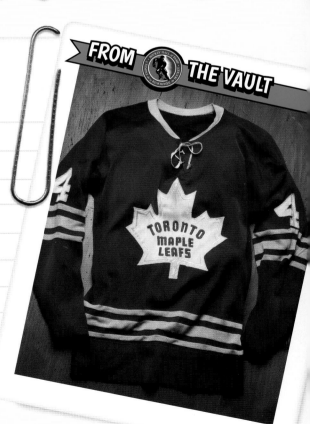

FROM THE VAULT

VIACHESLAV FETISOV

HOCKEY HALL OF FAME: 2001

Even if he never played in the NHL, Viacheslav Fetisov would be considered one of the greatest defensemen ever. "Slava," as he was known, was a big and strong defender who was also fast on his feet. He could shut down top forwards, and he had a knack for knowing when to pinch in from the blue line to create scoring chances. ▶

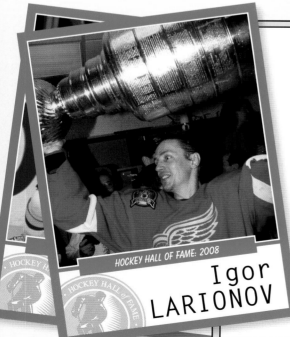

HOCKEY HALL OF FAME: 2008

Igor LARIONOV

THE RUSSIAN FIVE

Slava Fetisov and Igor Larionov were the top Russian stars of the 1980s. Larionov centered the famous KLM Line with Vladimir Krutov and Sergei Makarov. Fetisov and Alexei Kasatonov played defense with the trio, forming a dominant five-man unit for the Soviet national team. Larionov fought for the right to leave Russia and play in the NHL, and in 1989 the government let him and a few others go. Six years later, Fetisov and Larionov were reunited in Detroit where a new "Russian Five" was formed with Sergei Fedorov, Vyacheslav Kozlov and Vladimir Konstantinov. They won the Stanley Cup in 1997.

Fetisov was born in Russia, and he joined Moscow's Central Red Army junior team as a 16-year-old in 1974–75. In 1977 and 1978, he helped the Soviet Union (Russia) win the first two official World Junior Championships. He was named the Best Defenseman at the tournament in 1978 and was selected to the All-Star Team along with another future superstar, Wayne Gretzky. Fetisov was just 19 years old in 1978, but he played alongside grown men in the World Championships that year too. Remarkably, he was named the Best Defenseman at the Worlds. It was the first of six times he'd win that honor, and the first of seven times he'd help the Soviets win the World title! Fetisov made his first appearance at the Olympics in 1980. The United States won a surprising gold medal that year, with the Soviets taking silver. Fetisov later won

Olympic gold medals in 1984 and 1988. He also won the Golden Stick Award as the best player in Europe three times!

For many years, players from the Soviet Union were not allowed to leave Russia to join the NHL, but that changed, and in 1989 Fetisov finally got his chance. He was 31 years old when he joined the New Jersey Devils. He was traded to Detroit in 1995 where he was one of five Russian players that helped the Red Wings win the Stanley Cup in 1997 and 1998.

FROM RIVAL TO TEAMMATE

Larry Murphy's NHL career began with a bang when he recorded 76 points for Los Angeles in 1980–81. That's a rookie record for defensemen that still stands. Murphy went on to play 21 years in the NHL and ranks fifth all-time among defensemen with 1,216 points. In 1987, Murphy was a member of Team Canada when they defeated Slava Fetisov and the Soviet Union in a thrilling Canada Cup championship. Many people consider that to be the greatest tournament in hockey history. Ten years later, Murphy joined Fetisov in Detroit and helped the Red Wings win back-to-back Stanley Cups.

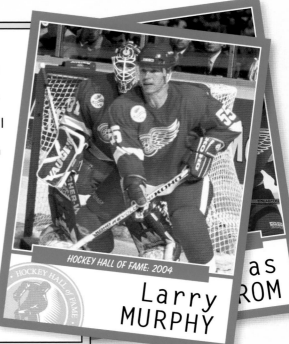

HOCKEY HALL OF FAME: 2004

Larry MURPHY

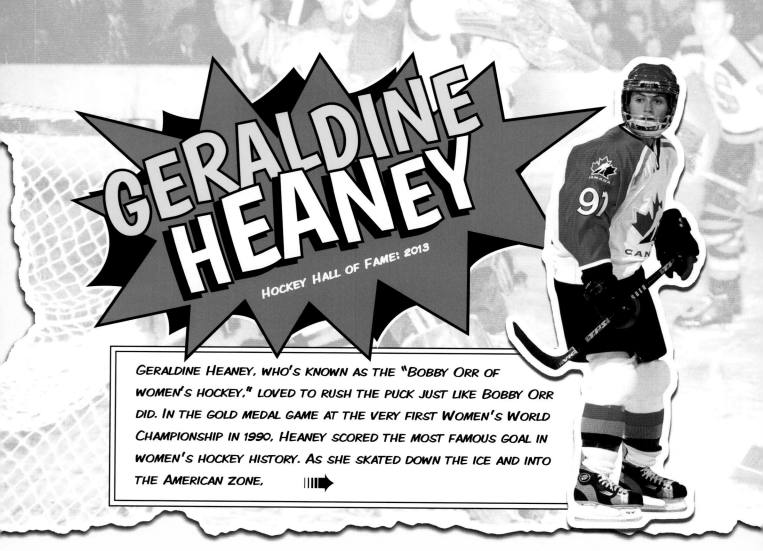

GERALDINE HEANEY

HOCKEY HALL OF FAME: 2013

GERALDINE HEANEY, WHO'S KNOWN AS THE "BOBBY ORR OF WOMEN'S HOCKEY," LOVED TO RUSH THE PUCK JUST LIKE BOBBY ORR DID. IN THE GOLD MEDAL GAME AT THE VERY FIRST WOMEN'S WORLD CHAMPIONSHIP IN 1990, HEANEY SCORED THE MOST FAMOUS GOAL IN WOMEN'S HOCKEY HISTORY. AS SHE SKATED DOWN THE ICE AND INTO THE AMERICAN ZONE, ▐▐▐▶

FROM THE VAULT

GOAL-SCORER'S DUDS

Geraldine Heaney wore this jersey with the Toronto Aeros in the National Women's Hockey League in 2003–04. It was Heaney's final season as a player and she ended the year in style. At the Esso Women's Nationals in March of 2004, the Aeros represented their home province as Team Ontario. In the championship game against Hayley Wickenheiser and Team Alberta, Heaney rushed end-to-end to score the winning goal for the Aeros at 3:39 of overtime. Making the play even more remarkable, Heaney was three months pregnant with her daughter Shannon at the time!

she split the U.S. defense and then lifted the puck over the goalie just before being knocked flying through the air. The goal gave Canada a 3–2 lead and sparked them to a 5–2 victory. Her goal was a lot like a goal scored by Bobby Orr to win the Stanley Cup in 1970. His is one of the most famous goals ever, and just like Heaney, Orr went flying through the air after he scored. Heaney's goal inspired many girls to play hockey, including future Team Canada star Cassie Campbell-Pascal. "When you're talking offensive defensemen in women's hockey," she once said, "Heaney's name will always be the one that comes up first."

Heaney was born in Northern Ireland, but she grew up in Toronto. When she was 13 years old in 1980, she began playing with the Toronto Aeros and she helped the team win six provincial championships over 18 seasons in the Ontario Women's Hockey Association. During that time Heaney was named the Most Valuable Defenseman three times!

Heaney represented Canada at the first seven Women's World Championships. She was the only Canadian player to appear in every one of those tournaments, and she helped Canada win a gold medal every time! The United States beat Canada at the first Winter Olympic tournament in 1998, but Heaney was back in 2002 to help Canada win Olympic gold that year in her last international event!

Did You Know?

GERALDINE HEANEY WAS THE ONLY PERSON TO PLAY IN EVERY CANADIAN WOMEN'S NATIONAL CHAMPIONSHIP FROM 1987 TO 2001.

Dynamite Teammates

ANGELA JAMES (HHOF: 2010)

In 2010, American Cammi Granato and Canadian Angela James were the first women to be inducted into the Hockey Hall of Fame. Like Geraldine Heaney, James grew up in Toronto. There were so few girls' hockey teams when she was young that James played with boys. When she got older, she led the Ontario Women's Hockey Association in scoring eight times! She also won six league MVP awards. During the 1990s, James and Heaney were teammates with the Toronto Aeros and with the Canadian national team.

GREAT GOALIES

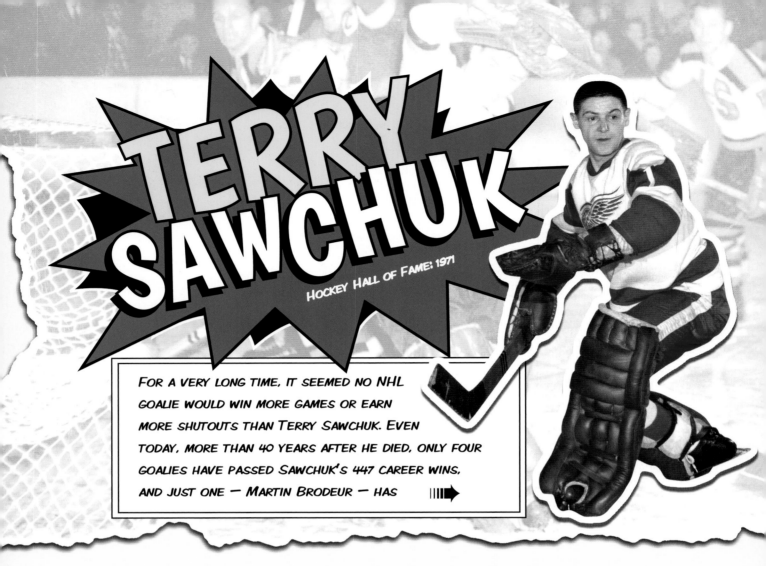

TERRY SAWCHUK

HOCKEY HALL OF FAME: 1971

FOR A VERY LONG TIME, IT SEEMED NO NHL GOALIE WOULD WIN MORE GAMES OR EARN MORE SHUTOUTS THAN TERRY SAWCHUK. EVEN TODAY, MORE THAN 40 YEARS AFTER HE DIED, ONLY FOUR GOALIES HAVE PASSED SAWCHUK'S 447 CAREER WINS, AND JUST ONE — MARTIN BRODEUR — HAS ▐▐▐▶

Blast FROM THE Past

GEORGE HAINSWORTH (HHOF: 1961)

George Hainsworth wasn't flashy. He didn't make diving saves or shout at other players. He just stopped the puck better than anyone else in his time. In 1928–29, Hainsworth recorded an amazing 22 shutouts in 44 games. He helped Montreal win the Stanley Cup in 1930 and 1931, and later reached the final twice while playing with the Toronto Maple Leafs. Hainsworth still ranks third in NHL history with 94 career shutouts. However, with the 10 shutouts he recorded while playing in the rival Western Hockey League, Hainsworth's professional total of 104 gives him more shutouts than Terry Sawchuk.

broken his record of 103 shutouts.

Sawchuk was a tense competitor and a person who found it hard to relax. Some of that was due to the nerves created by the scary task of stopping pucks without a mask. Some of it came from a hard childhood; two of Sawchuk's older brothers had died when he was a boy. When he was 10, he was given the goalie pads of his late brother Mike. By the time he was 16, he'd signed with the Detroit Red Wings. He became Detroit's starter in 1950–51 when he was 21.

Did You Know?

TERRY SAWCHUK WON THE VEZINA TROPHY THREE TIMES WITH DETROIT AND SHARED IT WITH JOHNNY BOWER IN TORONTO IN 1964–65.

Until then, goalies usually played a standup style, trying to keep their unmasked faces far away from the puck. But Sawchuk played differently, getting low to the ice in a deep crouch. It was dangerous, but he could see the puck better that way. In his first full NHL season, Sawchuk set a league record with 44 wins. He also led the league with 11 shutouts and was named rookie of the year. The next season, 1951–52, he posted 44 wins, 12 shutouts and led Detroit to the Stanley Cup! The Red Wings won the Cup again in 1954 and 1955, but Sawchuk was traded to Boston shortly after.

He was never happy in Boston and retired during the 1956–57 season. Boston traded him back to Detroit, where he spent seven more seasons before being moved to Toronto. In 1967, Sawchuk helped the Maple Leafs win the Stanley Cup.

THE RECORD BREAKER

When pucks were filling the nets in the high-scoring 1970 and '80s, Terry Sawchuk's long-held career NHL shutout record of 103 seemed safe. However, with the arrival of defensive-focused hockey in the 1990s, one potential record breaker emerged. Martin Brodeur played for the New Jersey Devils, one of the stingiest teams in the NHL, and he piled up as many as 12 shutouts a year. Brodeur broke Sawchuk's record with his 104th shutout in a win over Pittsburgh on December 21st, 2009. Brodeur finished his career with 125 shutouts, and also holds the NHL's wins record with 691 career victories.

9, 2001 008

Martin BRODEUR

nik ASEK

GLENN HALL

HOCKEY HALL OF FAME: 1975

GLENN HALL WAS SO GOOD, PEOPLE SIMPLY CALLED HIM "MR. GOALIE." DURING HIS 16 FULL NHL SEASONS, HALL EARNED SEVEN SELECTIONS TO THE LEAGUE'S FIRST ALL-STAR TEAM AND FOUR PICKS AS A SECOND-TEAM ALL-STAR. NO OTHER GOALIE IN NHL HISTORY HAS EVER HAD MORE THAN SIX ▐▌▶

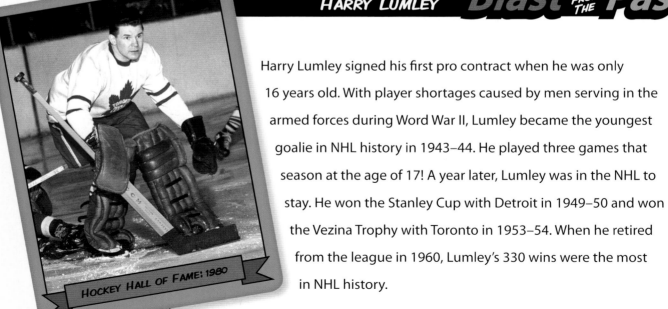

HARRY LUMLEY **Blast FROM THE Past**

HOCKEY HALL OF FAME: 1980

Harry Lumley signed his first pro contract when he was only 16 years old. With player shortages caused by men serving in the armed forces during Word War II, Lumley became the youngest goalie in NHL history in 1943–44. He played three games that season at the age of 17! A year later, Lumley was in the NHL to stay. He won the Stanley Cup with Detroit in 1949–50 and won the Vezina Trophy with Toronto in 1953–54. When he retired from the league in 1960, Lumley's 330 wins were the most in NHL history.

selections to the First Team, or eight All-Star honors overall!

As a rising star, Hall was part of the Detroit Red Wings organization where he learned from other star goalies Harry Lumley and Terry Sawchuk. Hall admired the way Sawchuk played in a low crouch when most other goalies used the stand-up style. But Hall took the move even further. He would spread his feet wide and drop to his knees while keeping his body upright. By doing so, he pioneered the "butterfly" style that Patrick Roy later refined. The move is still popular today! Hall was also known for a peculiar way of getting ready to play. He would get himself so worked up that he became sick to his stomach before almost every game. "I simply felt I played better when I got sick before a game," he said. "I hope it never bothered my teammates."

When Hall debuted in the NHL he impressed the Red Wings so much that Detroit traded Sawchuk to make room for him in 1955–56. He led the league with 12 shutouts that season and was named rookie of the year, but Detroit traded him to Chicago in 1957. The Black Hawks were the worst team in the NHL, but soon Hall helped make them great. Chicago won the Stanley Cup in 1960–61 and Hall won the Vezina Trophy for the first of three times in 1962–63. Hall spent his last four seasons with the St. Louis Blues.

THE REAL IRON MAN:
Glenn Hall's Streak

Glenn Hall holds one of the most amazing records in hockey history. Beginning at the start of the 1955–56 season and lasting until early in 1962–63, he played every single minute of every single game in goal for Detroit and Chicago for more than seven straight seasons! The streak stretched for 502 games, and reaches 552 games when the playoffs are counted. Making it all the more amazing, Hall played all those games without wearing a mask! The streak finally ended on November 7, 1962, when a back injury forced Hall out of action during the first period.

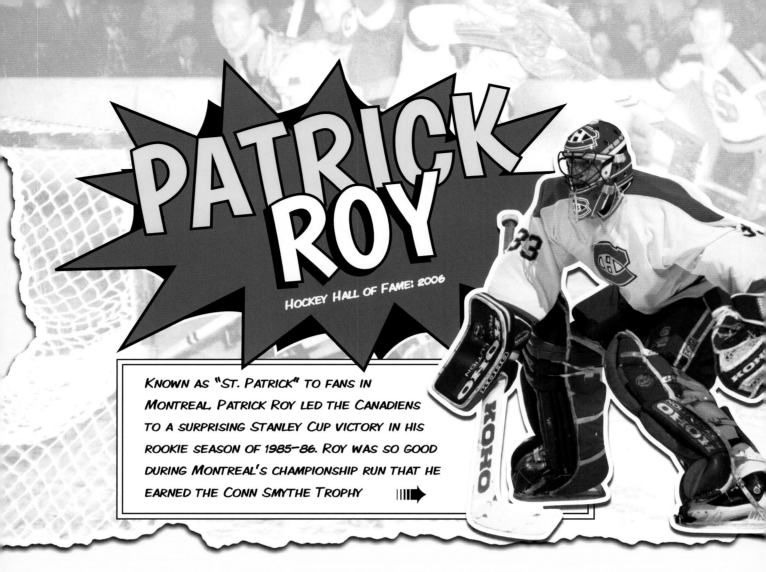

PATRICK ROY

Hockey Hall of Fame: 2006

KNOWN AS "ST. PATRICK" TO FANS IN MONTREAL, PATRICK ROY LED THE CANADIENS TO A SURPRISING STANLEY CUP VICTORY IN HIS ROOKIE SEASON OF 1985–86. ROY WAS SO GOOD DURING MONTREAL'S CHAMPIONSHIP RUN THAT HE EARNED THE CONN SMYTHE TROPHY ▌▌▌▶

AS THE NUMBER-one netminder in Montreal, Carey Price is part of a legendary legacy that includes Patrick Roy, Ken Dryden, Bill Durnan, Jacques Plante and Georges Vezina. Many people consider Price to be the best goalie in the world today. He backstopped Canada to a gold medal at the 2014 Winter Olympics and then had a huge season with the Canadiens in 2014–15. He set a franchise record with 44 wins and not only earned the Vezina Trophy, but also the Hart Trophy as NHL MVP. Price's next big step will be trying to win the Stanley Cup in Montreal.

MODERN MATCH
CAREY PRICE

as playoff MVP. At age 20, he was the youngest player ever to win the award. He would win it again with Montreal in 1993 and with the Colorado Avalanche in 2001, making him the only person in NHL history to be playoff MVP three times!

Roy had a lot of strange habits that fans found interesting. He would always hop over the blue lines when he skated across the ice, and he admitted to talking to his goal posts! In the net Roy seemed to be a bundle of nerves as he constantly bobbed his head up and down and craned his neck from side to side. What he was really doing was getting mentally ready by visualizing himself playing perfectly. Roy may have looked odd some times, but he was a true student of the game. He came to the NHL at a time when improvements in goalie equipment made it lighter and stronger. That helped Roy and his goalie coach Francois Allaire perfect the

"butterfly" style that allowed Roy to spread out low across the bottom of the net. His style influenced goalies all across his home province of Quebec and was soon copied by people all around the world.

Roy spent 18 full seasons in the NHL with Montreal and Colorado. He won the Vezina Trophy three times and was the winner of the Jennings Trophy five times. He won the Stanley Cup twice with the Canadiens and twice with the Avalanche and is the NHL's all-time playoff leader with 151 wins!

Did You Know?

PATRICK ROY SET AN NHL RECORD WITH 10 OVERTIME WINS IN THE 1993 PLAYOFFS TO LEAD MONTREAL TO THE STANLEY CUP.

Blast FROM THE Past

HAP HOLMES (HHOF: 1972)

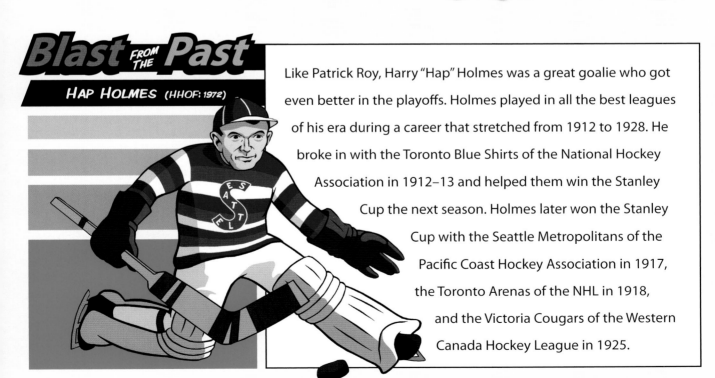

Like Patrick Roy, Harry "Hap" Holmes was a great goalie who got even better in the playoffs. Holmes played in all the best leagues of his era during a career that stretched from 1912 to 1928. He broke in with the Toronto Blue Shirts of the National Hockey Association in 1912–13 and helped them win the Stanley Cup the next season. Holmes later won the Stanley Cup with the Seattle Metropolitans of the Pacific Coast Hockey Association in 1917, the Toronto Arenas of the NHL in 1918, and the Victoria Cougars of the Western Canada Hockey League in 1925.

GEORGES VEZINA

HOCKEY HALL OF FAME: 1945

THE MONTREAL CANADIENS ARE THE OLDEST, STILL-OPERATING TEAM IN PROFESSIONAL HOCKEY. BUT WHEN THEY STARTED OUT BACK IN 1909-10, THE CANADIENS WEREN'T VERY GOOD. IN FACT, THEY FINISHED LAST IN THE NATIONAL HOCKEY ASSOCIATION (NHA) THAT SEASON. GOALTENDING WAS THEIR BIGGEST PROBLEM.

VEZINA TROPHY: 1994, 1995, 1997–1999, 2001
JENNINGS TROPHY: 1994, 2001, 2008

Dominik
HASEK

GOALIE TROPHIES

The Montreal Canadiens donated the Vezina Trophy to the NHL in 1926–27 in honor of Georges Vezina. For years, it was given to the goalie (or goalies) on the team that allowed the fewest goals each season. Since 1981–82, the Vezina has gone to the goalie that's voted to be the best in the league by the general managers of every NHL team. In 1981–82, a new trophy was donated to reward the goalies on the team allowing the fewest goals. The Jennings Trophy is named after William M. Jennings, a long-time executive with the New York Rangers.

The NHA season was just 12 games long, but the Canadiens tried four different goalies and the team won just two games. During that same season, Georges Vezina led his hometown Chicoutimi Hockey Club to a victory over the Canadiens in an exhibition game. After that, Montreal signed him for the 1910–11 season. Vezina went on to play every single game for the Canadiens for the next 15 years! He helped them win the Stanley Cup for the first time in 1915–16 and led the league in wins and goals-against average when the NHL began in 1917–18.

Vezina played a standup style and almost never dropped to the ice, even when the rules were changed to allow goalies to do so. He was always calm and cool under pressure, which led to his nickname, the "Chicoutimi Cucumber" (from the old expression "cool as a cucumber"). Vezina led the NHL in goals-against average again in 1923–24 and helped the Canadiens win another Stanley Cup that year. In 1924–25, he posted a career-best 1.81 goals-against average to lead the NHL one more time, but when the next season started, it was clear that something was wrong. Vezina looked weak in training camp and in the first game of the 1925–26 season, he was pulled after the first period. It turned out he was suffering from tuberculosis, a very serious lung disease. Vezina never played another game, and he passed away on March 27, 1926.

Did You Know?

GEORGES VEZINA POSTED THE FIRST SHUTOUT IN NHL HISTORY WITH A 9–0 VICTORY OVER TORONTO ON FEBRUARY 18, 1918.

Parallel Puckstopper

PADDY MORAN (HHOF: 1958)

Paddy Moran played his entire career during an era when hockey rules said a goalie had to remain standing at all times. As a result, his stats don't look very impressive to fans of today. Moran spent 12 seasons from 1905 to 1917 playing in the top hockey leagues of his day. He played 11 of those years with the Quebec Bulldogs and helped them win the Stanley Cup in 1912 and 1913. Unlike Georges Vezina, Moran was known for having a temper, and he would sometimes slash skaters who got too close to his net.

CLINT BENEDICT

Hockey Hall of Fame: 1965

Clint Benedict doesn't have a trophy named in his honor like old-time Montreal goalie Georges Vezina, but Benedict was probably the better goalie. Over the years that they played in the league together, Benedict's stats were almost always better. During the first 10 years after the NHL was formed in 1917–18, ▶▶▶

Percy LeSueur (HHOF: 1961) — Blast FROM THE Past

Percy LeSueur was the goalie Clint Benedict replaced in Ottawa. LeSueur joined the team late in the 1905–06 season. He couldn't help Ottawa hold on to the Stanley Cup that year, but he helped them win it again in 1909 and 1911. Decades before goalies wore blockers and catchers, LeSueur invented special goalie gloves that had very long cuffs. They were called "gauntlet gloves," and they gave goalies better protection. They were very popular in his era. He also designed a more modern style of goalie net that was used from 1912 to 1925.

Vezina had the league's best goals-against average three times, but Benedict led the league six times! He also led the league in wins six times during the first seven seasons and led (or shared the lead) in shutouts for seven straight seasons. No one else in history has led the NHL in shutouts more often!

Most importantly, Benedict was responsible for one of the biggest rule changes in NHL history. When the league started, goalies had to stay on their feet at all times. Benedict, though, always found a way to go down to stop the puck. When asked he'd say he was tripped, or that he "accidentally" fell. Midway through the very first NHL season, the league decided it was okay for goalies to drop to the ice. After that, Benedict spent so much time on his knees that people called him "Praying Benny."

Benedict joined the Ottawa Senators of the National Hockey Association (NHA) for the 1912–13 season when he was 20 years old. He took over as Ottawa's number-one goalie in 1914–15 and helped the Senators win the NHA championship. Benedict stayed with Ottawa when the NHA was re-formed into the NHL and helped the team win the Stanley Cup in 1920, 1921 and 1923! Before the 1924–25 season, the Senators sold Benedict to a new NHL team called the Montreal Maroons. In just their second season of 1925–26, Benedict helped them win the Stanley Cup.

Did You Know?

CLINT BENEDICT WAS THE FIRST NHL GOALIE TO WEAR A MASK. HE WORE A LEATHER MASK FOR A FEW GAMES DURING HIS FINAL SEASON OF 1929–30.

Parallel Puckstopper

HUGH LEHMAN (HHOF: 1958)

Hugh Lehman's pro career stretched from 1906–07 until 1927–28 when he was 42 years old! He spent his last two seasons with the Chicago Black Hawks, but Lehman played most of his career in leagues that pre-dated the NHL or were rivals to it. Lehman spent 13 seasons in the Pacific Coast Hockey Association from 1911–12 to 1923–24 and was a 10-time All-Star. He played for the Stanley Cup eight times in his career, but only won it once, with the Vancouver Millionaires in 1914–15 when they beat Clint Benedict and the Ottawa Senators.

JACQUES PLANTE

HOCKEY HALL OF FAME: 1978

JACQUES PLANTE WAS THE OLDEST OF 11 CHILDREN GROWING UP IN SHAWINIGAN, QUEBEC. THE FAMILY HAD SO LITTLE EXTRA MONEY THAT WHEN HE STARTED PLAYING HOCKEY THEY COULDN'T AFFORD TO BUY HIM A HOCKEY STICK. INSTEAD, PLANTE PLAYED WITH A STICK HIS FATHER CLEVERLY CARVED FROM A TREE ROOT! PLANTE LOVED HOCKEY AND HE BECAME ▎▎▎▶

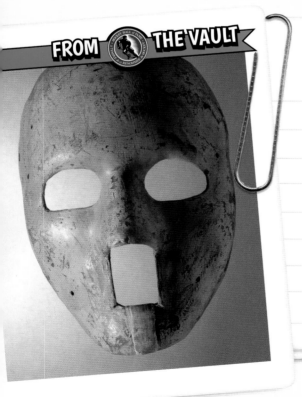

FROM THE VAULT

THE CHANGING FACE OF HOCKEY

Jacques Plante was the first goalie to regularly wear a mask. Aside from a few early experiments, goalies had always played bare-faced. People thought if a goalie wore a mask, he was showing the opposing team he was scared. Plante had been practicing with a mask since 1955, but his coach wouldn't let him wear it in games. Then, on November 1, 1959, Plante's nose was badly cut by a shot from Andy Bathgate of the New York Rangers. When Plante was stitched up and returned to action, he was wearing this mask. He vowed never to play again if he couldn't wear it regularly!

a real rink rat, hanging out at local arenas and getting into as many games as possible. By the time he was 20, Plante had signed with the Montreal Canadiens. The Canadiens had several goalies on the team ahead of him, but Plante was spectacular in a few brief appearances in the NHL. In 1954–55, the Canadiens made him their number-one goalie.

Plante always studied the game trying to find ways he could play better. He was one of the first goalies to roam from his crease, stopping dump-ins behind his net or racing out to play the puck to his defensemen. Sometimes, his daredevil ways made his coaches nervous, but it was obvious that Plante knew what he was doing. From 1955–56 to 1959–60, he helped the Canadiens win the Stanley Cup five years in a row and was also named the Vezina Trophy winner as the league's top

Did You Know?

JACQUES PLANTE LED THE LEAGUE WITH THE LOWEST GOALS-AGAINST AVERAGE A RECORD EIGHT TIMES DURING HIS 17-PLUS SEASONS IN THE NHL.

goaltender! He won the Vezina again in 1961–62 and also won the Hart Trophy that year as the NHL's MVP. It took 35 years before another goalie was named MVP.

Plante was traded to New York in 1963 and retired in 1965. After three seasons away from the game, he made a comeback with St. Louis in 1968–69. Plante won the Vezina Trophy for a record seventh time that year, sharing the award with teammate Glenn Hall. Plante continued to play until 1975, retiring for good when he was 46 years old!

GOALTENDING GURU

Jacques Plante was considered an oddball. He didn't socialize with his teammates and he relaxed by knitting toques and undershirts. But Plante understood goaltending and he was happy to teach others. Plante helped groom Bernie Parent for greatness when they became teammates in Toronto in 1971. He also gave tips to Vladislav Tretiak when the Soviet (Russian) National Team faced Team Canada in 1972. That same year, Plante wrote an instructional book on goaltending and later became the NHL's first goalie coach when he was hired by Philadelphia in 1977 to help his old teammate, Parent, find his form.

HOCKEY TIPS
FOR THE
GOALTENDER
BY JACQUES PLANTE

DOMINIK HASEK

Hockey Hall of Fame: 2014

MANY OF THE GREATEST GOALIES IN HISTORY HAVE INSPIRED IMITATORS. JACQUES PLANTE'S HABIT OF ROAMING FROM HIS CREASE IS NORMAL FOR GOALIES TODAY. TERRY SAWCHUK'S DEEP CROUCH LED TO GLENN HALL'S BUTTERFLY STYLE, WHICH WAS IMPROVED UPON BY TONY ESPOSITO AND PATRICK ROY.

Carey Price

HART OF THE MATTER:
Goalies and the MVP Award

When Dominik Hasek was named MVP in 1996–97, no goalie had won the Hart Trophy since Jacques Plante in 1961–62. Hasek received 50 of 54 first-place votes to win the award in a landslide. "The Dominator," as he was known, was nearly as dominant the next year, winning the Hart again with 43 first-place votes. Since Hasek, goalies Jose Theodore (2001–02) and Carey Price (2014–15) have also won the Hart. Before Hasek, Roy Worters (1928–29), Chuck Rayner (1949–50), Al Rollins (1953–54) and Plante were the only goalies to be named MVP.

Dominik Hasek, however, played a style so unique that no one has ever really copied him. If other goalies were butterflies, Hasek was more like a caterpillar. He was incredibly fit and so flexible that a TV commercial jokingly referred to his "having a slinky for a spine." Hasek flopped to the ice on almost every shot to cover the bottom of the net. Rolling and twisting in his crease, he made saves that seemed impossible. Sometimes he even dropped his stick so that he could cover the puck with either hand. Hasek was smart and studied the game very hard. He also had a competitive spirit that pushed him to be the best. Still, it took a while for him to get his chance in the NHL.

Hasek was chosen by the Chicago Black Hawks with the 199th pick in the 1983 NHL Draft. He remained at home in Czechoslovakia until 1990 and then spent two seasons mostly

in the minors, and occasionally as a backup in Chicago, before being traded to the Buffalo Sabres in 1992.

In nine seasons with the Sabres through to 2000–01, Hasek won the Vezina Trophy six times and was selected as a First-Team All-Star six times. He also became the first (and to date, only) goalie to win the Hart Trophy as NHL MVP twice, doing so in 1996–97 and 1997–98. Already a star in his homeland, Hasek solidified that status by leading the Czech Republic to an Olympic gold medal in 1998. Later, he won the Stanley Cup with Detroit in 2002 and 2008.

MODERN MATCH
HENRIK LUNDQVIST

MANY GOALIES FROM Europe have played in the NHL since Sweden's Hardy Astrom became the first in 1977. Astrom never was a star, but today there are top NHL goalies from many different countries. Currently, the best European is Sweden's Henrik Lundqvist. He joined the New York Rangers in 2005–06 and has been so good that people call him "King Henrik." Lundqvist was the first goalie in NHL history to win 30 games or more in each of his first seven seasons. Had it not been for the 2012–13 lockout, that string could have been 11 seasons long! He won the Vezina Trophy in 2011–12.

BERNIE PARENT

HOCKEY HALL OF FAME: 1984

BERNIE PARENT GREW UP IN MONTREAL IN THE 1950s AND LOVED PLAYING ROAD HOCKEY WITH HIS FRIENDS. PARENT CHEERED FOR THE MONTREAL CANADIENS AND IMAGINED HIMSELF MAKING SAVES JUST LIKE MONTREAL'S GOALIE JACQUES PLANTE. FOR PARENT, THE TRANSITION FROM ROAD HOCKEY TO ICE HOCKEY WAS DIFFICULT. ▐▐▐▶

Pelle LINDBERGH

THE SUCCESSOR

When he was just 20 years old, Pelle Lindbergh led Sweden to a bronze medal in hockey at the 1980 Winter Olympics. Still, his dream was to become the NHL's first great European goalie. Lindbergh's hero growing up was Bernie Parent, so he was very excited to be drafted by Philadelphia. Working with his idol as his goalie coach, Lindbergh became the Flyers' number-one goalie in 1982–83 and won the Vezina Trophy two years later. He was well on his way to realizing his dream when he died in a car accident early in the 1985–86 season.

but he practiced hard. Success was slow to come at first, but as he gained more experience he got better. By the time he was a teenager he was an NHL prospect. When Parent was 18 in 1963, he signed with the Boston Bruins. He played occasionally in Boston, and when the league added six new teams for the start of the 1967–68 season, the Philadelphia Flyers chose Parent to be their goalie.

After three and a half years in Philadelphia, Parent was traded to Toronto in 1971. The other Toronto goalie was Parent's hero, Jacques Plante. He was very excited. "I learned more from [Plante] in two years with the Leafs than I did in all my other hockey days," Parent said. He returned to the Flyers for the 1973–74 season, and very quickly proved he was the best goalie in the NHL. He led the league with 47 wins, 12 shutouts, and a 1.89 goals-against average that season. He was nearly as good in 1974–75, leading the league with 44 wins, 12 shutouts and a 2.03 average!

The Flyers played rough and took a lot of penalties, but Parent almost always made the saves they needed. Not only did he win the Vezina Trophy in 1973–74 and 1974–75, he led the Flyers to back-to-back Stanley Cups and won the Conn Smythe Trophy as playoff MVP both years! Parent was forced to retire after being hit in the eye with a stick in 1979.

Did You Know?

BERNIE PARENT POSTED A SHUTOUT IN THE DECIDING GAME OF THE STANLEY CUP FINAL WHEN PHILADELPHIA WON IT IN 1974 AND IN 1975.

PLAYOFF PAYOFF:
Goalies and the Conn Smythe Trophy

The Conn Smythe Trophy was first given to the MVP of the playoffs in 1965. Since then, more goalies have won the award than players at any other position. Bernie Parent was the first person to win it in back-to-back seasons, and goalie Patrick Roy is the only player to win it more than twice. Sometimes, the Conn Smythe is awarded to a player on the losing team. Five players have won the award on the losing side, and four of them are goalies: Roger Crozier (Detroit 1966), Glenn Hall (St. Louis 1968), Ron Hextall (Philadelphia 1987) and Jean-Sebastien Giguere (Anaheim 2003).

Jonathan Quick, 2012 Conn Smythe winner

JOHNNY BOWER

HOCKEY HALL OF FAME: 1976

IT HAS NEVER BEEN EASY TO MAKE IT TO THE NHL. AND IT WAS EXTRA HARD DURING THE ORIGINAL SIX ERA, WHEN FOR 25 SEASONS, FROM 1942–43 TO 1966–67, THE NHL HAD ONLY SIX TEAMS. FOR MOST OF THAT TIME TEAMS ONLY HAD ONE GOALIE ON THEIR ROSTER, WHICH MEANT THAT OF ALL THE GOALIES ▐▐▐▶

Parallel Puckstopper

GUMP WORSLEY (HHOF: 1980)

When Johnny Bower first played in the NHL with the New York Rangers in 1953–54, it was Gump Worsley he replaced. Worsley won his job back a year later, but New York was a bad team. Things got a lot better for Worsley when he was traded to Montreal in 1963–64. He won the Vezina Trophy twice and the Stanley Cup four times with the Canadiens. Worsley, whose real first name was Lorne, played his final seasons with the Minnesota North Stars. He refused to wear a mask until his last NHL season of 1973–74.

in the world only six were playing in the NHL. An awful lot of good goalies had to wait a long time for their chance at the NHL, and that only happened when another goalie retired, got injured or started playing poorly. For Johnny Bower, he waited patiently for twelve years before finally becoming a full-time NHLer.

Records today list Bower's birthday as November 8, 1924, but when he was playing nobody was really sure how old he was. When he was only 15, Bower lied about his age to join the Canadian Army during World War II. After that, he was shy to let anyone know his true age. He continued playing hockey after his time in the army and spent eight seasons with the Cleveland Barons in the American Hockey League (AHL) before finally getting a chance in the NHL. He played for the New York Rangers in 1953–54, but was back in the minors the next year.

Bower was named the AHL's best goalie and most valuable player three times each. He figured he'd spend the rest of his career in the minors, but was convinced to try his luck with the Toronto Maple Leafs in 1958–59 when he was 34 years old! His hard work had finally landed him a full-time job in the NHL. Over the next 11 seasons, Bower won the Vezina Trophy twice and helped Toronto win the Stanley Cup four times!

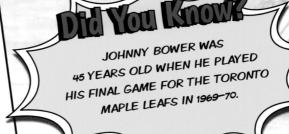

Did You Know?

JOHNNY BOWER WAS 45 YEARS OLD WHEN HE PLAYED HIS FINAL GAME FOR THE TORONTO MAPLE LEAFS IN 1969–70.

Blast FROM THE Past

CHUCK RAYNER (HHOF: 1973)

Chuck Rayner spent most of his NHL career on bad teams in New York. In fact, he played 10 years in the NHL and only made the playoffs twice! Still, in 1949–50, Rayner led the Rangers to the seventh game of the Stanley Cup Final. They lost to the Detroit Red Wings, but Rayner was rewarded for his excellent season by winning the Hart Trophy as league MVP. When Johnny Bower was breaking in with the Rangers, Rayner taught him to use the poke check. Diving headlong towards skaters was dangerous in the days before masks, but Bower made the gutsy check his signature move.

KEN DRYDEN

Hockey Hall of Fame: 1983

At 6-foot-4 (193 cm) and 205 pounds (93 kg), Ken Dryden wasn't just a big goalie, he was bigger than many players! Dryden was called up to the Montreal Canadiens late in the 1970-71 season and was a surprise starter when they faced Boston in the playoffs. The Bruins had enjoyed a record-shattering ▐▐▐▶

WHEN KEN DRYDEN put a stop to the Boston Bruins in round one of the 1971 playoffs, Phil Esposito compared his long arms and legs to an octopus. He also called Dryden a thieving giraffe. When Ben Bishop made his debut in 2008, he became the tallest goalie in NHL history at 6-foot-7 (201 cm). An American from Denver, Colorado, Bishop played university hockey before reaching the NHL, just as Dryden had done. He didn't have the same immediate success as Dryden, but after a trade to the Tampa Bay Lightning in 2013, Bishop has become a franchise goalie.

MODERN MATCH
BEN BISHOP

offensive season, and with the likes of Bobby Orr and Phil Esposito, Boston was expected to easily beat Montreal. But Dryden, who had only played in six NHL games, led the Canadiens to a stunning upset. When Montreal went on to win the Stanley Cup, Dryden was named the MVP of the playoffs!

The Canadiens had waited a long time for Dryden to make it to the NHL. It was rare for NHL hopefuls to attend university in those days, but Dryden spent four years at Cornell University in Ithaca, New York. He also played one year for Canada's national hockey team before finally joining the Canadiens. After his heroic playoff, Dryden officially became Montreal's number-one goalie in 1971–72, and because he played in so few games the previous year, he was still considered a rookie for that season. He went on to be named NHL rookie of the year!

Did You Know?

KEN DRYDEN'S AMAZING CAREER RECORD OF 258–57–74 GIVES HIM A LIFETIME WINNING PERCENTAGE OF .758. THAT'S BY FAR THE BEST IN NHL HISTORY!

In 1972–73, Dryden won the Vezina Trophy for the first time and Montreal won the Stanley Cup again.

While he was playing for the Canadiens, Dryden was also attending school to become a lawyer and sat out the entire 1973–74 season to finish his studies. When he returned to the Canadiens in 1974–75, the team was about to become one of the greatest in hockey history. Montreal won the Stanley Cup four years in a row from 1976 to 1979 and Dryden won the Vezina Trophy every year!

Blast FROM THE Past BILL DURNAN

Ken Dryden only played eight seasons in the NHL, but he won the Vezina Trophy five times and the Stanley Cup six times. Bill Durnan's career in Montreal 25 years earlier was amazingly similar. Durnan starred with the Canadiens for seven seasons from 1943 to 1950. Montreal won the Stanley Cup twice during those years and Durnan won the Vezina Trophy six times! Durnan was ambidextrous, which means he could use his left or right hand equally well. He had special goalie gloves designed that allowed him to hold his stick or catch the puck with either hand.

HOCKEY HALL OF FAME: 1964

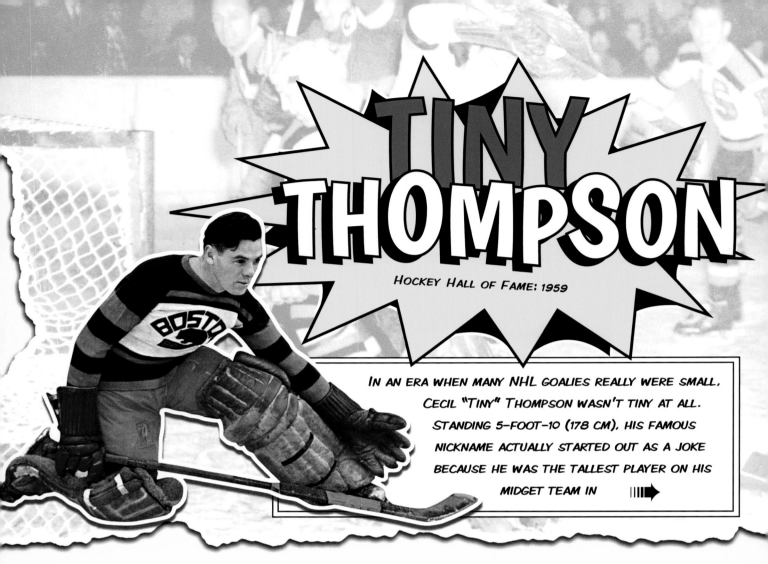

TINY THOMPSON

HOCKEY HALL OF FAME: 1959

IN AN ERA WHEN MANY NHL GOALIES REALLY WERE SMALL, CECIL "TINY" THOMPSON WASN'T TINY AT ALL. STANDING 5-FOOT-10 (178 CM), HIS FAMOUS NICKNAME ACTUALLY STARTED OUT AS A JOKE BECAUSE HE WAS THE TALLEST PLAYER ON HIS MIDGET TEAM IN ▐▐▐▶

Parallel Puckstopper

ROY WORTERS (HHOF: 1969)

There was no joking when it came to Roy Worters' nickname. Standing 5-foot-3 (160 cm) and weighing only 135 pounds (61 kg), Worters was known as "Shrimp." He may have been small, but he was a big talent! Worters played on bad teams his whole career, but did his best to keep them competitive. In 1928–29, he became the first goalie in NHL history to win the Hart Trophy as league MVP! Only two teams scored fewer goals than his New York Americans that year, but Worters' 13 shutouts and 1.15 goals-against average got them into the playoffs.

Calgary, Alberta. And once he got to the NHL, the term "Tiny" best described his goals-against average!

Thompson began his NHL career with the Boston Bruins in 1928–29. In his first game, he earned a shutout in a 1–0 win over the Pittsburgh Pirates. Thompson went on to post 12 shutouts that season and had a goals-against average of 1.15. That season was the lowest-scoring season in NHL history, and Thompson's average ranked second in the league behind George Hainsworth. In the playoffs, Thompson out-dueled

Hainsworth with two more shutouts when Boston swept Montreal in the semifinals. The Bruins then swept the New York Rangers to win the Stanley Cup for the first time!

The next season, 1929–30, the NHL introduced new passing rules that led to more scoring. Still, Thompson's 2.19 goals-against average was the best in the league, and he won the Vezina Trophy for the first time. He led the NHL in wins as well, as Boston had an amazing record of 38–5–1 during the 44-game regular season. That year, however, Hainsworth and the Canadiens got their revenge in the playoffs when Montreal upset Boston to win the Stanley Cup.

Thompson was a four-time All Star and he won the Vezina Trophy four times in his career, which was a league record when he retired from the NHL in 1940.

Did You Know?

PAUL THOMPSON OF THE RANGERS BECAME THE FIRST NHL PLAYER TO SCORE AGAINST HIS OWN BROTHER WHEN HE BEAT TINY THOMPSON ON MARCH 18, 1930.

ROBERTO LUONGO, LIKE Tiny Thompson, earned his puck-stopping reputation early in his career. Unlike Thompson, though, Loungo built his reputation playing on bad teams. In his first NHL game he stopped 43 shots for the New York Islanders. He later spent time playing with the Florida Panthers where he regularly faced the most shots in the league. Luongo played eight seasons with the Vancouver Canucks, leading them all the way to Game 7 of the 2010 Stanley Cup Final. He also backstopped Canada to a gold medal at the 2010 Olympics. Luongo is now stopping pucks in Florida again.

MODERN MATCH
ROBERTO LUONGO

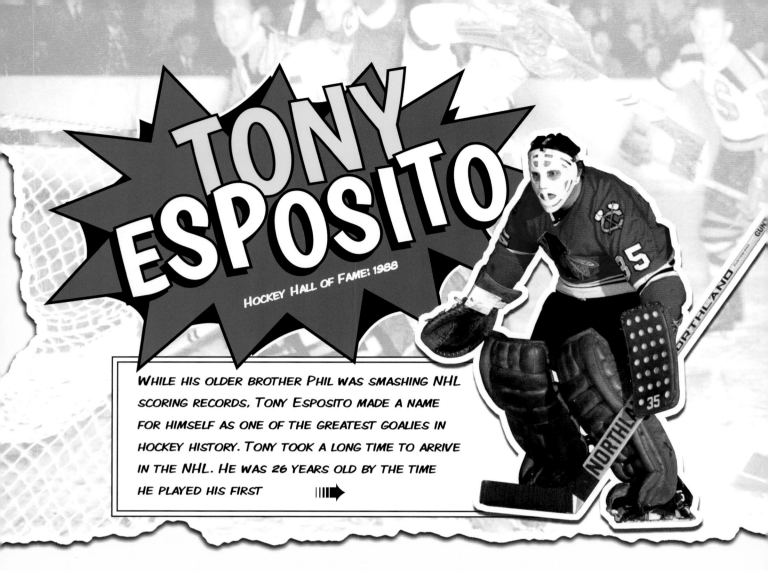

TONY ESPOSITO

HOCKEY HALL OF FAME: 1988

WHILE HIS OLDER BROTHER PHIL WAS SMASHING NHL SCORING RECORDS, TONY ESPOSITO MADE A NAME FOR HIMSELF AS ONE OF THE GREATEST GOALIES IN HOCKEY HISTORY. TONY TOOK A LONG TIME TO ARRIVE IN THE NHL. HE WAS 26 YEARS OLD BY THE TIME HE PLAYED HIS FIRST ▶

Parallel Puckstopper

ROGIE VACHON (HHOF: 2016)

Rogie Vachon was called up to Montreal during the 1966–67 season and shared goaltending duties with Gump Worsley. Together they won the Vezina Trophy in 1967–68 and helped the Canadiens win the Stanley Cup that year and the next. Montreal had many goaltending options, which is why prospects like Tony Esposito ended up in Chicago and Vachon wound up playing in Los Angeles. Only 5-foot-7 (170 cm) but an acrobat in the net, Vachon became a star with the Kings during the 1970s. His No. 30 jersey was the first in Kings history to be retired.

full season in 1969–70. Today, that would make him too old to win the Calder Trophy as rookie of the year, but back then it would have been crazy to give the award to anybody else.

Though he came from Sault Ste. Marie, Ontario, Esposito was one of the first big stars to make it to the NHL from an American college. After three stellar seasons at Michigan Tech University, he signed with the Montreal Canadiens in 1967. Esposito saw a bit of action with the team in 1968–69, and even got his name engraved on the Stanley Cup when the Canadiens won it that year. But Montreal had a lot of great goalies. They didn't hang on to Esposito, and the Chicago Black Hawks picked him up. Goalies almost always wore No. 1 or No. 30 in those days, but Esposito wanted something to make himself stand out, so he asked to wear No. 35. However,

Did You Know?

TONY ESPOSITO SHARED THE NET WITH KEN DRYDEN ON TEAM CANADA DURING THE 1972 SUMMIT SERIES AGAINST THE SOVIET UNION.

the numbers that really stood out during the 1969–70 season were the spectacular statistics he had. Esposito led the NHL with 15 shutouts that season. Nobody had posted that many in more than 40 years, and nobody has done so since. Esposito won both the Vezina and the Calder Trophies that season. He later won the Vezina Trophy two more times. Playing with his legs spread wide and relying on a lightning-fast glove hand, Esposito went on to become the fourth goalie in NHL history to record 400 career wins.

George Hainsworth

1928–29:
The Year of the Shutout

The 1928–29 season was the lowest-scoring season in NHL history. The two teams playing on any given night combined to score an average of less than three goals per game. In addition to George Hainsworth's 22 shutouts, seven other goalies had 10 or more shutouts that season. Hainsworth led the league with a 0.92 goals-against average, but the starting goalies on the other nine teams in the league all had averages ranging from 1.15 to 1.85. At one point during the season, the Chicago Black Hawks went eight straight games without scoring a single goal!

VLADISLAV TRETIAK

HOCKEY HALL OF FAME: 1989

VLADISLAV TRETIAK WASN'T SUPPOSED TO BE THAT GOOD. IN 1972 HIS SOVIET (RUSSIAN) NATIONAL TEAM PLAYED AGAINST THE TOP STARS FROM THE NHL IN AN EIGHT-GAME TOURNAMENT CALLED THE SUMMIT SERIES. THE RUSSIAN TEAM HAD DOMINATED INTERNATIONAL HOCKEY SINCE THE 1960S BUT HAD NEVER PLAYED AGAINST NHL PLAYERS.

FROM THE VAULT

WORLD CLASS JERSEY

In league play in Russia, Vladislav Tretiak helped the Red Army win 13 championships in 14 seasons from 1970 to 1984. He was a First-Team All-Star every season! Internationally, Tretiak played at the World Championships 13 times and won 10 World titles. He also played at the Olympics four times, winning three gold medals and one silver. In all, he played 98 international games and posted a goals-against average of 1.78. Tretiak wore this jersey at the 1973 World Championship in Moscow. The Russians were a perfect 10-and-0 that year and won the World title.

They were expected to lose badly against the mighty Canadians. Instead, Canada narrowly escaped defeat.

Before the series, Team Canada sent scouts to watch the Russians. The game they saw Tretiak play was on the night before he got married. He didn't stop many shots. "I couldn't concentrate on the game," he later admitted. The scouts reported that Tretiak was the weakest Russian player. But in reality, Tretiak was one of the best goalies in the world. His stellar play in the Summit Series made him incredibly popular, even in Canada. Back then, Russians weren't allowed to leave their country to play in the NHL, but the Montreal Canadiens tried for years without success to bring him over.

Tretiak was only 15 years old when he began practicing with Moscow's Central Red Army, the top team in Russia. Two years later,

in 1969–70, he became the team's starting goalie. Tretiak made his first appearance at the World Championships in 1970 and at the Olympics in 1972. He starred with the Central Red Army and the national team until 1984. The Russians were nearly unbeatable in those years, and they played many exhibition games against NHL teams too. On New Year's Eve in 1975, Tretiak led the Red Army to a 3–3 tie with the Montreal Canadiens despite being outshot 38–13. Many people consider this to be the greatest game ever played.

NO RUSSIAN GOALIE has ever really come up to the standard set by Vladislav Tretiak in his day. Among the best to follow in his footsteps are Nikolai Khabibulin and Evgeni Nabokov, who both won more than 300 games during their NHL careers. However, only one Russian goalie has ever won the Vezina Trophy. Sergei Bobrovsky won the award with the Columbus Blue Jackets in 2012–13, and was also named to the First All-Star Team that season. Bobrovsky set Blue Jackets franchise records in 2012–13 with a 2.00 goals-against average and a .932 save percentage.

MODERN MATCH

SERGEI BOBROVSKY

ED BELFOUR

HOCKEY HALL OF FAME: 2011

No one in the NHL wanted Ed Belfour after his junior hockey career. He wasn't drafted into the NHL, but that didn't stop him from trying to make the pros. Finally, after leading the University of North Dakota to the NCAA ▐▐▐▶

Parallel Puckstopper

Tom Barrasso

A few years before Ed Belfour won both the Calder Trophy and the Vezina Trophy, Tom Barrasso did the same thing when he broke into the NHL with the Buffalo Sabres in 1983–84. Amazingly, Barrasso was just 18 years old that season and joined the NHL directly from high school! Barrasso was traded to Pittsburgh early in the 1988–89 season and helped the Penguins win the Stanley Cup in 1991. They won it again in 1992, beating Belfour and the Blackhawks that year. Barrasso is a member of the United States Hockey Hall of Fame.

championship in 1986–87, he signed with the Chicago Blackhawks.

In 1990, the Blackhawks hired Russian goalie legend Vladislav Tretiak to coach their goalies. Belfour worked with Tretiak at training camp and won the job as Chicago's starting goalie. He went on to have one of the greatest seasons any rookie goalie has ever had. Belfour played 74 out of 80 possible games and set a club record that still stands with 43 wins! He led Chicago to the best record in the NHL and also led the league with a 2.47 goals-against average. Not only did Belfour win the Calder Trophy as the NHL's best rookie, but also the Vezina Trophy as the league's best goalie. His win marked only the fourth time a goalie had won both awards in the same season. Belfour led Chicago to the Stanley Cup Final the following year, and won the Vezina Trophy again in 1992–93.

Belfour was a hard worker who expected nothing but the best effort, every night, from himself and his teammates. Sometimes, that demanding attitude made him hard to get along with. Chicago traded Belfour to San Jose in 1997 and the next season he signed with the Dallas Stars. Belfour posted a career-best 1.88 goals-against average with the Stars in 1997–98 and won the Stanley Cup with them in 1999. He ended his career with the Florida Panthers in 2006–07. His 484 wins rank him third all-time in NHL history.

Did You Know?

AFTER LEAVING CHICAGO, ED BELFOUR WORE NO. 20 IN HONOR OF HIS FORMER GOALIE COACH AND HALL OF FAMER, VLADISLAV TRETIAK, WHO'D WORN NO. 20 DURING HIS CAREER.

UNDRAFTED HALL of FAMERS

For most future NHL stars, their career begins with the excitement of hearing their name called at the NHL Draft. The NHL held its first draft in 1963, and since then, nearly every player who has been inducted to the Hockey Hall of Fame has been drafted … but not all of them! Ed Belfour is the only undrafted goalie currently in the Hall of Fame. Borje Salming and Peter Statsny were never drafted either, but signed as free agents from Europe. American Joe Mullen and Canadians Dino Ciccarelli and Adam Oates are the only other undrafted Hall of Famers.

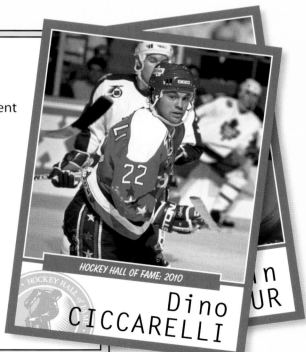

HOCKEY HALL OF FAME: 2010

Dino CICCARELLI

TURK BRODA

HOCKEY HALL OF FAME: 1967

TURK BRODA WAS THE FIRST GOALIE IN NHL HISTORY TO WIN 300 GAMES. THOUGH HIS CAREER ENDED MORE THAN 60 YEARS AGO, HIS 302 VICTORIES ARE STILL THE MOST IN THE HISTORY OF THE TORONTO MAPLE LEAFS. IN FACT, JOHNNY BOWER HAS THE SECOND-MOST WINS OF ANY OTHER MAPLE LEAFS' ▐▐▐▶

RILEY HERN (HHOF: 1962)

Blast FROM THE Past

Like Turk Broda, Riley Hern had a reputation for winning championships. Hern played in the early 1900s when hockey players first got paid to play the game. Pittsburgh was the center of pro hockey in those days, and Hern helped the Pittsburgh Keystones win the American championship in 1901–02. He later won two more U.S. titles with another team. When Canadian teams began to pay their players in 1906–07, Hern returned to his home country. He joined the Montreal Wanderers and helped them win the Stanley Cup in 1907, 1908 and 1910!

goalie, and he is still 83 behind Broda! Good as he was during the regular season, Broda was even better in the playoffs. He led the Maple Leafs to five Stanley Cup championships and boasted a goals-against average of 1.98 in 101 career playoff games.

Broda's real first name was Walter. The most common story about how he got the nickname "Turk" is that the large freckles he had when he was a boy looked like the spots on a turkey egg. Broda grew up in Brandon, Manitoba, and attracted the attention of scouts from Detroit while playing in Brandon and Winnipeg in the early 1930s. In 1936, the Maple Leafs bought Broda from the Red Wings for almost $8,000! That may not seem like much money today, but it was a huge price to pay for a minor-league goalie during The Great Depression.

Many people thought the Leafs had been

Did You Know?

IN 1941–42, TURK BRODA BECAME THE FIRST TORONTO GOALIE TO WIN THE VEZINA TROPHY. HE WON IT AGAIN IN 1947–48.

cheated, but Broda soon won over the fans in Toronto with his outgoing personality. His hard work in practice impressed his teammates. After the team reached the finals in 1938, 1939 and 1940, Broda and the Maple Leafs won the Stanley Cup in 1942. He later spent two years with the Canadian Army in World War II, and when he returned to Toronto he led the Maple Leafs to the most successful time in team history. They won the Stanley Cup three years in a row from 1947 to 1949, and then won it again in 1951.

TOO BIG TO FAIL:
Broda's Battle of the Bulge

Turk Broda didn't really look like an athlete, but despite his chubby appearance he was a hard worker. Even so, when Toronto struggled early in the 1949–50 season, Maple Leafs owner Conn Smythe ordered Broda out of the lineup until he lost some weight. Newspapers loved the story of Broda's "Battle of the Bulge." They showed pictures of him sitting on a scale while eating a steak or drinking juice for dinner while trying to lose weight. Broda was back after a week of dieting and went on to post nine shutouts that season, which was a career high.

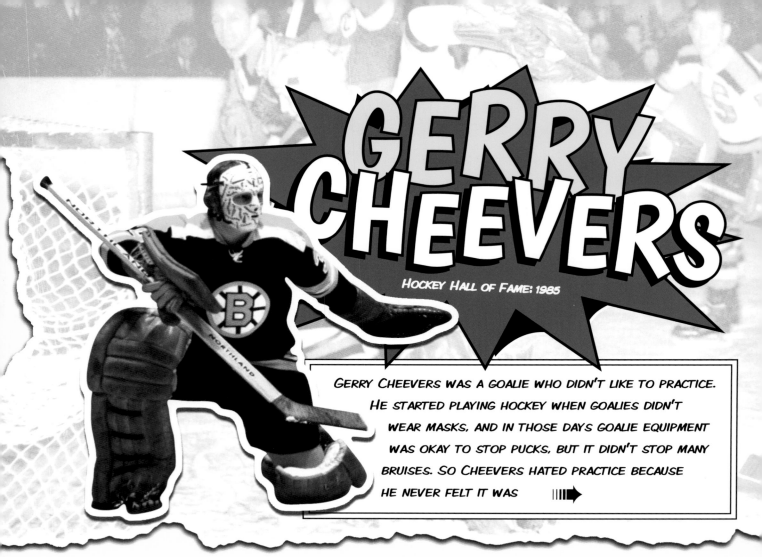

GERRY CHEEVERS

HOCKEY HALL OF FAME: 1985

GERRY CHEEVERS WAS A GOALIE WHO DIDN'T LIKE TO PRACTICE. HE STARTED PLAYING HOCKEY WHEN GOALIES DIDN'T WEAR MASKS, AND IN THOSE DAYS GOALIE EQUIPMENT WAS OKAY TO STOP PUCKS, BUT IT DIDN'T STOP MANY BRUISES. SO CHEEVERS HATED PRACTICE BECAUSE HE NEVER FELT IT WAS ||||➤

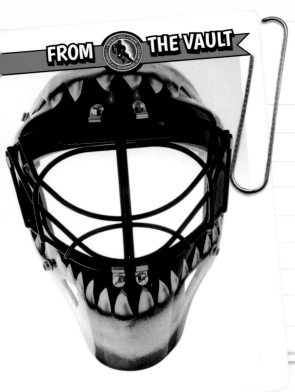

FROM THE VAULT

PAINTED MASKS

Former NHL goalie Brian Hayward wore this mask while playing with the San Jose Sharks in 1992–93. The first goalie to feature a design on his mask was Gerry Cheevers. Cheevers was faking an injury to get out of practice after taking a soft shot in the face. As a joke, he had the trainer paint a line of stitches onto his white, fiberglass mask. It got a big laugh, so every time Cheevers got hit in the face, he added more stitches. Over the years, the black stitch-marks on Cheevers' mask became his trademark.

worth the risk of getting hurt. When Cheevers was young he also liked to roam from his net to play the puck. His coach with the St. Michael's Majors hated this. To try and teach Cheevers a lesson, the coach made him play a handful of games as a left winger during the 1960–61 season. "I was never so happy to get back in goal!" Cheevers said afterward.

Cheevers was slated behind Johnny Bower and Terry Sawchuk on the Toronto Maple Leafs roster and only played briefly with the Leafs before he was picked up by Boston in 1965. Cheevers shared the Bruins' net with veteran Eddie Johnson, who helped him adjust to life in the NHL. Soon, Cheevers took over as the team's number-one goalie. The Bruins were the worst team in the league at the time, but the addition of Bobby Orr, Phil Esposito and others turned them around in a hurry! Cheevers still didn't like to practice, but he earned a reputation as a goalie who played his best when it mattered most, helping Boston win the Stanley Cup in 1970 and 1972. During the 1971–72 season, Cheevers set a record that still stands by playing 32 games in a row without a loss. He had 24 wins and eight ties during his streak.

Cheevers helped the Bruins reach the Stanley Cup Finals again in 1977 and 1978. He retired after the 1979–80 season and spent the next four-and-a-half seasons as Boston's coach.

Did You Know?

GERRY CHEEVERS WAS ONE OF THE FIRST NHL SUPERSTARS TO LEAVE THE LEAGUE AND JOIN THE RIVAL WORLD HOCKEY ASSOCIATION IN 1972–73.

MODERN MATCH
TUUKKA RASK

AFTER A STELLAR junior career in his native Finland, Tuukka Rask began his NHL career as property of the Toronto Maple Leafs before joining the Bruins, just like Gerry Cheevers. Toronto took Rask in the first round of the 2005 NHL Draft, but traded him to Boston one year later. After spending one more year in Finland, Rask joined the Bruins for the 2007–08 season and got his first NHL win against the Maple Leafs! Rask led the NHL in goals-against average during the 2009–10 season and won the Vezina Trophy in 2014.

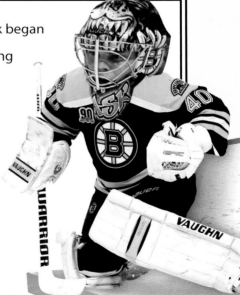

BILLY SMITH

HOCKEY HALL OF FAME: 1993

BILLY SMITH WAS NEVER VERY POPULAR, AT LEAST AS FAR AS THE OPPOSITION WAS CONCERNED. KNOWN AS "BATTLING BILLY," SMITH NEVER HESITATED TO SWING HIS STICK AT THE ANKLES OF ANY OPPONENT WHO GOT TOO CLOSE TO HIS CREASE. WHEN HIS TEAM LOST A PLAYOFF SERIES, ▐▐▐➤

Parallel Puckstopper

RON HEXTALL

On November 28, 1979, Billy Smith became the first goalie in NHL history to be credited with scoring a goal. In reality, Smith was simply the last Islander to touch the puck before a Colorado Rockies player accidentally shot it into his own open net. The first goalie to actually shoot the puck the length of the ice and score into an open net was Ron Hextall of the Philadelphia Flyers on December 8, 1987. Like Smith, Hextall was an aggressive goalie who often swung his stick at opponents and sometimes got into fights with other goalies.

Smith often skipped the ritual of shaking hands with the other team. He would yell at referees and even at his own teammates (sometimes), but that was usually just to fire them up. Mostly, though, Billy Smith battled to stop the puck, and he was pretty good when it came to that!

The Los Angeles Kings originally selected Smith in the 1970 NHL Draft. After spending most of the next two years in the minors, he was picked up by the New York Islanders. Smith struggled with his new team for the first two seasons, but the Islanders quickly became a contender and Smith emerged as New York's number-one goalie in 1974–75. He usually shared playing time — first with Glenn "Chico" Resch and later with Rollie Melanson and Kelly Hrudey — however, when the playoffs rolled around, it was Smith the Islanders counted on.

By the end of the 1970s, the Islanders had developed a reputation as a top team in the regular season that always seemed to struggle in the playoffs. That all changed in the spring of 1980. That year, Smith played in 20 of the Islanders' 21 playoff games and helped them win the Stanley Cup. It was the first of four straight championship seasons for Smith and the Islanders. During those years, Smith played 72 playoff games and posted a record of 57–13! He won the Conn Smythe Trophy as playoff MVP during the team's final Stanley Cup run in 1983.

Did You Know?

BILLY SMITH WAS THE FIRST GOALIE TO WIN THE VEZINA TROPHY WHEN NHL GENERAL MANAGERS BEGAN TO VOTE FOR THE AWARD IN 1981–82.

DOUBLE THE FUN:
The Two-Goalie System

Before the 1965–66 season, NHL teams only had to dress one goalie for every game. Some teams began using a backup goalie as early as the 1920s, but it was pretty common for teams to use the same goalie all season long. Even when teams did use a backup, it was usually because their regular starter had suffered a serious injury. However, from the mid 1960s until the end of the 1980s, the "two-goalie system" became very popular. Like the New York Islanders, who rotated Billy Smith and Glenn Resch, most teams carried two or three goalies.

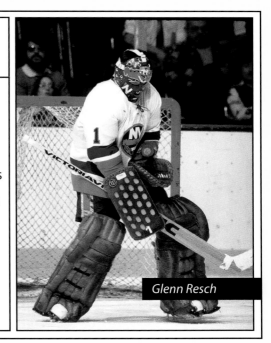

Glenn Resch

GRANT FUHR

HOCKEY HALL OF FAME: 2003

WHEN GRANT FUHR ARRIVED IN THE NHL WITH THE EDMONTON OILERS IN 1981–82, GOAL SCORING WAS AT AN ALL-TIME HIGH. FUHR'S TEAMMATE WAYNE GRETZKY NOTCHED A RECORD 92 GOALS THAT SEASON AND LED THE NHL WITH 212 POINTS! FUHR WAS JUST 19 YEARS OLD, BUT ▸

SCORING TODAY IS nothing like it was when Wayne Gretzky starred for Edmonton. Still, playing on a Pittsburgh team that features Sidney Crosby, Evgeni Malkin and Phil Kessel, people often compare Marc-Andre Fleury to Grant Fuhr. Pittsburgh made Fleury the first pick in the 2003 NHL Draft, which is rare for a goalie. Like Fuhr, Fleury made his first NHL start as a 19-year-old and was soon ranked among the top goalies in the NHL. During game seven of the Stanley Cup Final in 2009, Fleury made a spectacular diving save with two seconds left to preserve Pittsburgh's victory.

MODERN MATCH
MARC-ANDRE FLEURY

he won 28 games and lost only five. He became the youngest goalie in NHL history to play in the All-Star Game and finished third in voting for rookie of the year. He was second behind Billy Smith in voting for the Vezina Trophy.

Playing with the high-scoring Oilers, Fuhr didn't always get a lot of help from his defense. His goals-against average was usually high, but he gained a reputation as someone who rarely let the other team score the big goal. Fuhr might give up four in a game, but only if Edmonton scored five or more. If the game was close, opponents found it almost impossible to beat Fuhr for the goal they needed to tie it up or go ahead. Edmonton's all-out attack helped Fuhr set an NHL record for goalies with 14 assists in 1983–84 while his goaltending helped the Oilers win the Stanley Cup that season. They

Did You Know?

GRANT FUHR SET A RECORD FOR NHL GOALIES BY PLAYING 79 GAMES IN A SINGLE SEASON WHEN HE DID SO FOR THE ST. LOUIS BLUES IN 1995–96.

won it again three times over the next four years!

Fuhr won the Vezina Trophy in 1987–88 but his play slipped the following season and he later admitted to using drugs. Fuhr worked hard to recover and he played backup for Edmonton when they won the Stanley Cup in 1989–90. He was traded in 1991, and played for five teams over the next nine years, always putting up solid numbers. Though injuries finally slowed him down in his final season of 1999–2000, Fuhr became just the sixth goalie in NHL history to top 400 wins!

Parallel Puckstopper

ANDY MOOG

Andy Moog joined the Oilers in 1980–81 and led them to a stunning playoff upset of Montreal that spring. From 1982–83 through 1986–87, Moog shared netminding duties in Edmonton with Grant Fuhr. But, when it came time for the playoffs, Moog spent most of his time on the bench. He was traded to Boston in 1988 and later played for Dallas and Montreal before retiring in 1998. Though Moog was overshadowed by bigger names throughout his career, his regular-season record of 372–209–88 ranks him among the most successful goalies in NHL history!

FRANK BRIMSEK

HOCKEY HALL OF FAME: 1966

A FEW DAYS BEFORE THE 1938–39 SEASON, BRUINS GOALIE TINY THOMPSON SUFFERED A BAD CUT ABOVE HIS RIGHT EYE. FRANK BRIMSEK WAS CALLED UP FROM THE MINORS AND OPENED THE SEASON WITH TWO STRAIGHT WINS. THOMPSON RETURNED TO THE NET AFTER THAT, BUT BRUINS BOSS ART ROSS LIKED WHAT HE'D SEEN OF THE NEW YOUNG ROOKIE. ▮▮▮▶

Blast FROM THE Past

ALEX CONNELL (HHOF: 1958)

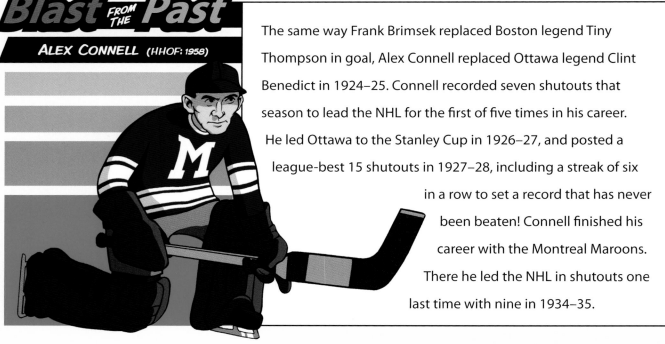

The same way Frank Brimsek replaced Boston legend Tiny Thompson in goal, Alex Connell replaced Ottawa legend Clint Benedict in 1924–25. Connell recorded seven shutouts that season to lead the NHL for the first of five times in his career. He led Ottawa to the Stanley Cup in 1926–27, and posted a league-best 15 shutouts in 1927–28, including a streak of six in a row to set a record that has never been beaten! Connell finished his career with the Montreal Maroons. There he led the NHL in shutouts one last time with nine in 1934–35.

A few weeks later, he traded Thompson to Detroit and made Brimsek his goaltender. Boston fans, and even some of the players, weren't sure about the move. There was some grumbling when Brimsek lost his first game, but he bounced back with three straight shutouts. After a 3–2 win in his next game, Brimsek recorded three more shutouts. In his first eight games as an NHL regular, Brimsek had seven wins and six shutouts! He'd be known as "Mr. Zero" from then on.

Brimsek finished the 1938–39 season with a record of 33–9–1, leading the league with his 33 wins, 10 shutouts and 1.56 goals-against average. Brimsek became the first goalie in NHL history to win the Vezina Trophy as best goalie and the Calder Trophy as rookie of the year in the same season. He also led the Bruins to the Stanley Cup. Brimsek would never have another season quite as amazing as his first, but he still had plenty of success. Brimsek and the Bruins won the Stanley Cup again in 1940–41 and he won a second Vezina Trophy in 1941–42.

Over his first eight seasons in the NHL, Brimsek was named either a First-Team or Second-Team All-Star every year. Making the streak even more incredible is the fact that after his first five years, Brimsek missed the next two seasons while serving with the United States Navy during World War II. He then had three more All-Star seasons.

Did You Know?

FRANK BRIMSEK BECAME AN ORIGINAL MEMBER OF THE UNITED STATES HOCKEY HALL OF FAME WHEN IT OPENED IN HIS HOMETOWN OF EVELETH, MINNESOTA, IN 1973.

MODERN MATCH: JONATHAN QUICK

IT WAS RARE to find an American-born player in the league when Frank Brimsek played in the NHL. Today, Jonathan Quick is one of about a dozen American goalies playing in the league. He became the number-one goalie for the Los Angeles Kings in 2008–09. During the 2011–12 season, Quick led the NHL with 10 shutouts and was second with a 1.95 goals-against average. When the Kings won the Stanley Cup that year, he was named the most valuable player of the playoffs. Quick has represented the United States at the Olympics in 2010 and 2014.

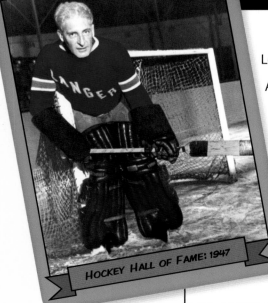

EDDIE GIACOMIN

HOCKEY HALL OF FAME: 1987

WHEN HE WAS 15 YEARS OLD, EDDIE GIACOMIN ATTENDED A JUNIOR TRYOUT FOR THE DETROIT RED WINGS. A SCOUT SENT HIM BACK HOME TO SUDBURY, ONTARIO, TELLING HIM HE WASN'T GOOD ENOUGH. "HE SAID I'D NEVER MAKE IT," GIACOMIN REMEMBERED. "HE SAID I SHOULD FORGET ABOUT BEING A GOALIE." GIACOMIN DIDN'T FORGET. HE WORKED HARD AND GOT ▌▌▌➡

HOCKEY HALL OF FAME: 1947

LESTER PATRICK — Blast FROM THE Past

Lester Patrick was a big name in hockey, but he wasn't really a goalie. As a star player from 1903 to 1926, he mostly played defense. From 1926 until 1947, he was the coach and general manager of the New York Rangers. A few times during his playing career, Patrick made emergency appearances in goal. Still, it was a shock when the 44-year-old coach took over in the Rangers net midway through Game 2 of the 1928 Stanley Cup Final. The team's regular goalie had been injured, and Patrick led the Rangers to a 2–1 victory in overtime!

a little help from his older brother, Rollie. A minor-league team in Washington wanted Eddie's older brother to come and play the last few games of the 1958–59 season, but Rollie didn't want to go. He sent Eddie instead, and it was the start of six full seasons that the younger Giacomin played in the minor leagues. Finally, Eddie got his chance in the NHL with the New York Rangers in 1965–66. The Rangers weren't a very good team. They missed the playoffs that year for the seventh time in eight seasons, but Giacomin was sharp and

he took over the number-one job in the Rangers' goal the next year. He was the busiest goalie in the NHL in 1966–67, playing 68 games during the 70-game season and leading the NHL with 30 wins and nine shutouts. The Rangers made the playoffs, and Giacomin was selected as a First-Team All-Star! During the eight full seasons he spent as the starting goalie in New York, the Rangers never missed the playoffs and Giacomin helped them reach the Stanley Cup Final in 1972.

Like Jacques Plante, Giacomin made acrobatic saves and liked to roam from the crease to play the puck. Unlike Plante, he didn't like wearing a mask because he thought he saw the puck better without one. Giacomin only started wearing a mask in 1970. He had a great season in 1970–71, sharing the Vezina Trophy with his backup goalie Gilles Villemure.

Did You Know?

THE RANGERS RETIRED EDDIE GIACOMIN'S NO. 1 IN 1989, MAKING HIM JUST THE SECOND PLAYER IN TEAM HISTORY TO HAVE HIS NUMBER RETIRED.

RANGER LEGENDS

Eddie Giacomin never won a Stanley Cup. In fact, the Rangers went without a Stanley Cup win for 54 years from 1940 to 1994! Goalie Mike Richter was one of the Rangers' heroes in 1993–94. After having shared the net with John Vanbiesbrouck since joining the team in 1989, Richter was handed the number-one job in 1993–94. He set a franchise record with 42 wins and was also the winning goalie in all 16 playoff victories the Rangers posted as they won the Stanley Cup! Richter was the first goalie to win 300 games with the Rangers. His No. 35 was retired in 2004.

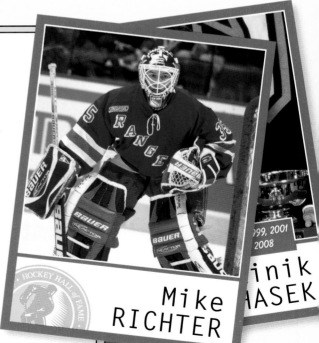

Mike
RICHTER

CHARLIE GARDINER

HOCKEY HALL OF FAME: 1945

WHEN CHARLIE GARDINER PLAYED HE WAS OFTEN THE BEST PLAYER ON HIS TEAM — AND EVEN THE BEST PLAYER ON EITHER TEAM! IF HIS CAREER HADN'T BEEN CUT TRAGICALLY SHORT AFTER JUST SEVEN SEASONS, IT'S POSSIBLE GARDINER MAY HAVE BECOME THE GREATEST GOALIE OF ALL TIME.

GARDINER WAS BORN IN EDINBURGH, ▮▮▮▶

IT TOOK COREY Crawford a while to establish himself in Chicago. The Blackhawks chose him in the second round of the 2003 NHL Draft, but he didn't become the team's starting goalie until the 2010–11 season. That year he was named to the NHL's All-Rookie Team. In 2012–13 he and Ray Emery combined to help Chicago win the Jennings Trophy for allowing the fewest goals. In the playoffs, Crawford was the main man in net as Chicago won the Stanley Cup! He won 13 games in the 2015 playoffs for his second Cup victory.

MODERN MATCH
COREY CRAWFORD

Scotland, but came to Canada at the age of seven and grew up in Winnipeg. Often known as "Chuck" instead of Charlie, he rose through the hockey ranks in his new hometown. When he was 21, Gardiner turned pro with the minor-league Winnipeg Maroons. Two years later, in 1927–28, he was on the NHL's Chicago Black Hawks. The Black Hawks were only in their second season, and they were bad. Gardiner always had to make plenty of big saves to keep his team in the game, and while Chicago usually lost, Gardiner was often praised for his fine play. People also liked his positive attitude. He was often heard shouting encouragement to teammates or joking with fans. After two dreadful seasons, Gardiner led Chicago to the playoffs in 1929–30. In 1930–31, the Black Hawks reached the Stanley Cup Final, but lost to Montreal. Still, the best — and

the worst — was yet to come.

Gardiner won the Vezina Trophy in 1931–32 and won it again in 1933–34. That year, he led Chicago to the final once again. This time they beat Detroit to win the Stanley Cup with Gardiner earning a shutout in overtime in the last game. Unfortunately, Gardiner had played much of that season with a badly infected tonsil in his throat. He ignored the pain, but the infection spread throughout his body. Back home in Winnipeg after the season, Gardiner collapsed and was rushed to the hospital. He died on June 13, 1934 at the age of 29.

Blast FROM THE Past — BOUSE HUTTON (HHOF: 1962)

Like Charlie Gardiner, Bouse Hutton had a short career but the reasons for it were very different. Hutton played hockey at a time in Canada when players had to be amateurs — they weren't allowed to be paid to play sports. When Hutton accepted money to play lacrosse in 1904, he had to give up his hockey career. Hutton played in his hometown of Ottawa from 1899 to 1904 and helped the "Silver Seven" win the Stanley Cup in 1903 and 1904. He also won national championships with Ottawa teams in lacrosse and football.

INDEX

INDEX

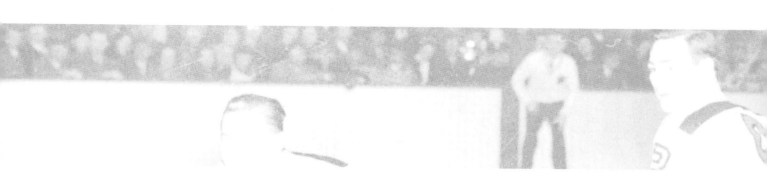

PHOTO CREDITS

T=Top, B= Bottom, BL=Bottom left, BR=Bottom right

All illustrations © George Todorovic

All images on covers, chapter openers and the introduction are listed below as they appear in the book.

Hockey Hall of Fame

Graphic Artists: 18T, 36T, 36B, 38T, 38B, 54T, 68BL, 68BR, 70T, 76T, 82T, 84T, 112T, 114B, 116T, 120T, 122T

Paul Bereswill: 10T, 14T, 26T, 30T, 42T, 44T, 86T, 92T, 132B

HHOF: 28, 64T, 104T, 106T, 118T, 121B, 136B

Dimaggio Kalish: 131B

Doug MacLellan: 7B, 20B, 40T, 51B, 62T, 81B, 102T, 104B, 124B, 125B, 133B

Matthew Manor: 16B, 26B, 45B, 59B, 65B, 94T, 95B, 101B, 108B, 128B

Mecca: 14BR

O-Pee-Chee: 30B, 112B, 128T, 130B

Portnoy: 14BL, 22T, 28B, 33B, 39B, 44B, 60T, 68T, 87B, 120B, 130T

Frank Prazak: 136T

Chris Relke: 10B, 50T, 56T, 124T

Hal Roth: 21B, 34B, 41B, 72B, 79B, 91B, 94B, 122B

Dave Sandford: 20T, 25B, 31B, 32T, 34T, 46B, 48T, 58T, 66T, 74T, 78T, 80T, 80B, 88T, 92B, 93B, 99B, 110T, 137B

Le Studio du Hockey: 10T, 29B

Imperial Oil–Turofsky: 16T, 17BL, 17BR, 62B, 70B, 72T, 89B, 90T, 98T, 100T, 100B, 108T, 114T, 117B, 126T, 127B, 134T, 138T

Icon Sportswire

Robin Alam: 35B

Chris Austin: 67B

Dustin Bradford: 18B

Justin Berl: 111B, 132B

Matt Cohen: 77B

Jerome Davis: 102B

Andrew Dieb: 10B,

Rich Graessle: 32B, 83B

Kathleen Hinkel: 24BL

Rich Kane: 20BR

Fred Kfoury III: 58B, 60B, 64B, 129B

Jeanine Leech: 15B, 22B, 27B, 40B, 47B, 73B, 86B

Mark LoMoglio: 50B, 63B, 116B

Jason Mowry: 123B

Minas Panagiotakis: 57B

Brad Rempel: 78B

Gary Rothstein: 119B

Juan Salas: 75B

Marc Sanchez: 110B

Ric Tapia: 42B, 48B, 85B, 88B, 135B

Chris Williams: 69B

Warren Wimmer: 138B

Getty Images

Melchior DiGiacomo: 46T